Tee Up Your Retirement

Tee Up Your Retirement

Avoid Common Financial Traps and
Put Yourself on the Green

STEVE ANZUONI

EXPERT PRESS

Tee Up Your Retirement:

Avoid Common Financial Traps and Put Yourself on the Green

Additional material Copyright © 2020 Steve Anzuoni
Copyright © 2018 Steve Anzuoni
All rights reserved.

Printed in the United States of America.

Steve Anzuoni
Fairway Financial, Inc.
508-398-3337

www.fairwayfinancial.net

ISBN-13: 978-1-946203-28-1

Contents

2020 Update

The SECURE Act

SINCE THIS BOOK WAS WRITTEN, there has been a major change to retirement law. In December 2019, the Setting Every Community Up for Retirement Enhancement (SECURE) Act was passed by the Congress and signed into law.

The Secure Act is the biggest change to retirement legislation in decades. I've been in business for over 33 years, and this law is having the greatest effect on my clients since the Roth IRA came about in 1996.

The SECURE Act is going to affect millions of Americans in planning for retirement when it comes to taxes, deductions, beneficiaries, legacy planning, and more. You need to learn how to make the most of these changes for you and your family.

The key to taking advantage of the SECURE Act, as with any law, is proactive planning.

What does the SECURE Act do?

As I reviewed the new law, I identified three major changes that can have a big impact on people between the ages of 55 and 75. There are a few other changes that will have some minor impacts, but these are the three major changes that will affect most retirees:

- The required minimum distribution (RMD) age has been raised to age 72. *(NOTE: this updates information in Chapters 3, 5, 7, and the Appendix.)*

- Individuals working past age 70 can now contribute to a deductible IRA.
- The stretch-IRA provisions for non-spouse beneficiaries have been eliminated.

Let's take a look at each of these in detail.

Raising the RMD age

Since the beginning of individual retirement arrangements (IRAs) in the '70s, the RMD age has always been 70 and a half. What this means is that, technically, you must take a minimum distribution from your IRA by April 1 of the year following the year you turn age 70 and a half.

Here's an example. Under the old rule, if you turned 70 in May, you would reach age 70 and a half in November, and you could defer your minimum distribution until April 1 of the following year. Then you would have to take another distribution for that tax year.

With the SECURE Act, all that has changed. The required minimum distribution age is now 72. No more half years, it's all pretty straightforward.

At age 72 you must take your distribution. There is a grandfathering provision, and the key date is Dec. 31, 2019. If you did not reach age 70 and a half by Dec. 31, 2019, you now can defer your RMD to age 72. If you had already turned 70 and a half by that date, then you have to abide by the old rule.

Basically, this means anybody born in 1950 or later will fall under the new rules. If you were born before June 30, 1949 then you will still have the old rules.

So what does all this mean for you? It gives you another year and a half of growth on tax-deferred assets like IRAs, 401(k)s, and 403(b)s before you have to take your minimum distribution.

The RMD is set by the IRS. They establish a table of guidelines that determine the minimum you must take. This is how the government begins to collect the taxes that you have deferred and deducted over all those years. That's why it's called the required minimum. Some people take only the minimum distribution because they don't need any more income, while others take more because they need additional income to supplement their Social Security and/ or pensions.

The raising of the RMD age allows more time for your assets to grow, but that's not all. Apart from the further deferral of taxes, I see an even bigger planning opportunity here.

I see a way to defer even more in the long term, by means of a Roth conversion.[1]

Roth conversions are a way for people to pay taxes today, at potentially lower rates, and never again have to pay taxes on that money or its potential growth. Would you be interested if I were to ask, would you like to pay taxes one time to potentially never have to pay income taxes on that IRA again, and never even have to take distributions anymore?

Most people would say yes to that. It's a great opportunity.

Let's look at an example. Let's say Bob is going to retire at age 67. He has been making $100,000 annual salary, but when he retires his income is going to drop by $40,000. His Social Security and his pension are going to provide $60,000, and he's okay with living on that reduced income. Bob also has an IRA that is worth $200,000. Under the old law, he would have to start taking his RMD from that IRA at age 70 and a half. Bob could let that IRA sit until that time, or he could say, "Now that my income has dropped by $40,000, why don't I take $40,000 out of that IRA and move it to a Roth? I pay the same income tax rate I was paying when I was working, but once I pay it the money has the potential to grow tax-free forever."

Think of the opportunity. Under the old law Bob only had about three years to make that conversion. Now, under the new law, he has five years to do that. In five years, converting $40,000 from his IRA each year, he will take care of his entire $200,000 IRA. And at age 72, if he needs income, Bob can now take the income from the Roth and not have it count against his Social Security tax, federal taxes, or state taxes.

It's unbelievable control. You can literally just take a whole pile of taxable money and disinherit the IRS. To me, that is the planning opportunity. It's another two years to move a tax-deferred account, pay income taxes on it now at potentially lower rates, and make it a tax-free account for life. That's planning opportunity number one from the SECURE Act.

Working past age 70

The second major change—and opportunity—from the SECURE Act is this: If you are still working after age 70, you can now contribute to a deductible IRA, provided you meet the income requirements—meaning that you don't make too much money.

During your working years, you can put money into a deductible IRA, subject to some limits. Before this change, the maximum age for contributing to a traditional deductible IRA was age 70 and a half. The SECURE Act eliminates that maximum age.

What might that mean for you in your retirement planning? Suppose you're someone like me, who is so happy in your work that you want to keep working into your 70s and perhaps beyond. That's going to be me; I know it. I'm going to be one of those guys who are going to just keep working.

So let's say I turn 70. At the point I take my maximum Social Security because there's no incentive for me not to take it. Let's also say I'm fortunate enough to have a pension. In spite of all that, I still like my job and I want to work. Suppose I make another $40,000. Now I'm eligible to make a deductible IRA contribution, which I could not do under the old law.

Under the current law right now, everybody age 50 and over can make a $7,000 deductible IRA contribution. The income phase out, if you're single, is $65,000 to $75,000. Beyond that phase out, you can no longer deduct that contribution. If you're married, filing jointly, the phase out is $104,000 to $124,000, so it's pretty liberal. If you're making less than that phase out, as a married couple, you are allowed to deduct an IRA contribution. This is for tax year 2020.

This change is pretty cool. But now it gets better. Let's say you put $7,000 in each year and you work for five more years, to age 75. That means you now have $35,000 that you have deducted by the time you stop working at age 75. What happens? Your income drops by $40,000 or $50,000, whatever your work is. At that point we can do what we call a backdoor IRA. You make a deductible contribution and then a few years later you turn around and exercise a Roth conversion on that money, just as we talked about in opportunity number one.

Elimination of the stretch IRA provision

We've described two really big positive changes—wonderful opportunities—from the SECURE Act, but I feel this third change will have the biggest impact for retirement planning.

The SECURE Act eliminates the stretch IRA provision for nonspousal beneficiaries, with a few exceptions, and will now require payouts to not exceed 10 years.

This is the bombshell. I call it the wealth tax.

This rule change is for all you folks out there—and I'm one of you—who feel like the middle class is always paying for everybody.

The elimination of the stretch IRA rule really applies to what I like to call wealth trusts, these dynasty trusts. By that I mean extralarge IRAs, those $1,000,000 and up. Let me set the stage.

Let's say hypothetically that John has a $1,000,000 IRA. John is 70 years old, he's not married, and his primary beneficiary is his 40-year-old son, Mike. John doesn't need a lot of the money from the IRA. He takes his minimum distributions until he dies 15 years later. Because John's investments did well and outpaced his minimum distributions, his IRA is now worth $1,500,000. Mike, who is now 55 years old, inherits that IRA, but if he takes that $1,500,000 in a lump sum, he's going to get absolutely crushed with the highest tax bracket possible. Under the old law, Mike could stretch that IRA over his life expectancy, his lifetime.

That's roughly 30 years. Think about that. Mike could literally take $50,000 a year from that account for the rest of his life and only have to pay taxes on $50,000 of it at a time. Under the old law, John was able basically to create a pension plan for his son.

That's not possible anymore under the SECURE Act. In my opinion, this law closed a loophole for the wealthy by saying that non-spouse beneficiaries must take the distribution over a maximum of 10 years.

The reason I call it the wealth tax is that it really affects the mega-IRAs and mega-401(k)s, those with $1,000,000 and up. If someone has a $200,000 IRA with one child as a beneficiary, the likelihood is that the beneficiary is going to take that money sooner. They're not likely to spread out $200,000, because it might only be worth $7,000 a year. Bit an IRA with $1,000,000 might be worth $50,000 a year, and the beneficiary might be more apt to spread that out. That's why those with the mega-401(k)s and mega-IRAs are the ones who need to do some proactive planning and learn how to do the IRA rescue plan, which I call the new stretch IRA. They're the ones who are going to get hit the hardest.

The new law still allows a pension plan to pass on to a spouse, and I agree with that completely. IRAs, 401(k)s and 403(b)s were initially designed as a supplemental retirement plan for the owner and his or her spouse. That was the original purpose. Then the limits went up, and people started putting in thousands and thousands of dollars a year. Right now, if you're over 50 years old, you can put $26,000 a year into these 401(k)s.

People took advantage of that opportunity. They maxed out their contributions and now they have these mega-IRAs and mega-401(k)s. The result was a lot of IRA trusts and attorneys planning to stretch out the money and create these dynasties. The government finally stepped in to stop this via the SECURE Act.

Let's go back to John and his son Mike. Under the new law, Mike, who's now age 55, must take his newly-inherited $1,500,000 over 10 years. He can take it in any way he wants—he doesn't have to do 10 equal payments—but over 10 years it must be gone.

That is a massive change, and for anybody out there who has these large IRAs, it's going to affect you greatly. It's going to have a major impact on what we call legacy planning. If you have an IRA trust, the odds are that it's now completely obsolete.

Having said that, it's not entirely bad news. Why not? As always, the key is proactive planning. I have been doing this for over 33 years, showing people how to create income-tax-free estates using discounted dollars. It's called life insurance. What life insurance offers is leverage. It's you paying pennies on the dollar. How does someone with $1 million IRA now plan a legacy for their kids? What we do is rescue that IRA, and here's how. We turn that $1 million IRA into $1 million in life insurance.

Here's an example. We all can make gifts of $15,000 a year for 2020. If you're married, you could do $30,000 a year per recipient. If you have two children, you could give away $60,000 a year to your kids, who do not have to pay taxes on that gift. You can report it as a deduction on your estate, not a deduction on your income tax, but a reduction in your estate for future taxes.

Now, let's face it, most people don't have $60,000 a year to give away. Maybe a couple might be able to do that between them. But suppose you have a $1 million IRA. If you took $15,000 a year, or as a couple, $30,000, from that IRA and used life insurance to make it worth $1 million at the second death, you could do a better job than the old law, because now your kids would inherit $1 million of tax-free cash that they can take however they want. They could spread it out over their lifetime or take it all at once; it's still tax free. You must be able to qualify for life insurance based on your health, but having certain conditions doesn't automatically disqualify you.

If you set this up right, there's no probate either, which is another plus. So the SECURE Act does have a major effect on large IRAs and 401(k)s, but with proper planning, you can take what seemed to be a negative change in the law and turn it into an even better legacy for your beneficiaries.

This IRA rescue strategy can be a better way to leave a legacy for your kids and at the same time disinherit the IRS. Think of it this way: How would you like to exhaust your IRA down to nothing and replace it all with tax-free money?

This is basically how it works. You make a contribution of up to $15,000 as an individual, or $30,000 as a couple. You can consider it a gift, but instead of making that gift directly to say your child—your beneficiary—you make the gift to a life insurance policy, and that life insurance policy is going to be worth the value of the IRA but it will be worth it tax free.

Let's say Don and Carol have a $1 million IRA from which they're taking income. Don dies and Carol keeps taking that income. When Carol dies, there might be some left over in the IRA, but the goal is to get the IRA spent down on the parents' lower tax bracket and then pass $1 million to their children tax free. Who wouldn't want to do that?

Get a financial check-up

Are you ready for the SECURE Act? This new law has brought us these great planning opportunities and I'm very excited to be able to add this to my already existing book.

Given these big changes, though, I feel that everybody out there needs to get a checkup. If you had a health change, you would go to your doctor and get a checkup. Well, right now you've got a financial change in your life and you need a financial checkup to see exactly how these new rules can benefit you and your family in the most tax-efficient way possible.

To me, this is the most amazing opportunity since the Roth IRA in the '90s. I want everybody out there to get this information right away, and that's why I took this occasion to add it to my book.

[1] *Determining when or if you should convert to a Roth IRA is an individual decision based on factors such as your financial situation, age, tax bracket, current assets, and alternative sources of retirement income. Your unique circumstances determine what is appropriate for you.*

Introduction:

If We Fail to Plan, We Plan to Fail

WHY DID YOU PICK UP THIS BOOK? Here's my guess: You're getting close to retirement and are concerned about not having saved enough. Maybe you've already retired, and you are concerned you might outlive your money, and have to go back to work at age 75 or even 80.

How do I know that? Because I'm in my mid-50s and I have those same fears and concerns. In America today, the number one fear for pre-retirees is not having saved enough for retirement, and the number one fear among retirees is outliving their income. Every time I conduct a seminar—and I've done hundreds of them—and I ask that question of my audience, it's not just the number one answer; it's the only answer.

It's a big concern. People are living longer and that puts a greater stress on their retirement resources. A retirement portfolio that may have been expected to produce income over 10-15 years now may have to do so for 20-30 years. I have clients now who are in their 90s, and they're still active. Check out the chart on the next page. It's truly an eye opener.

I want to make sure you don't outlive your money, and to do that, you need to have a plan, an **income** plan. We need to use the right tools—tools that will provide the right result, which is lifetime guaranteed **INcome**, not **IFcome**. You will learn the difference by reading this book.

How Long Must Your Money Last?

Living Longer in Retirement: Life Expectancy at Age 65

A healthy 65 Year Old Female has a 50% Chance of Living Beyond Age 90, or 25 More Years

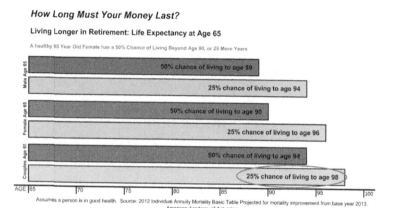

Assumes a person is in good health. Source: 2012 Individual Annuity Mortality Basic Table Projected for mortality improvement from base year 2013. American Academy of Actuaries

When I sit down with you to help you develop your plan, we will talk about your life style and goals. Then we discuss how we can make those goals and dreams a reality by building the right income buckets for your plan using your Social Security, a pension if you have one, and your retirement accounts such as your 401(k), IRA, and/or your 403(b) plans.

This is a process, and that's something most people don't understand: it's a **retirement income process**, one that continues before and during retirement.

I want to use my 30-plus years of knowledge and experience to help you understand the retirement income process and take the steps you need to achieve your retirement goals.

I started out in 1986 in the insurance business with John Hancock. When I began, I was offering life insurance and annuities, mostly to families. My job was to visit the homes of existing John Hancock clients and educate them about what they owned, and to offer more products in line with what they were trying to accomplish.

I worked extremely hard, became one of the top producers in that office, and ended up moving to a different office in Boston. Over the next 10 years I was recognized as one of the top five percent of Hancock's producers in the country.

In 1998, I read a book that truly changed my perspective on retirement and insurance planning. It was called *The 21st Century Agent*.

After I read the book, I set it on the table, looked at my wife, and said, "Honey, I'm leaving John Hancock and starting my own company."

She said, "But we have an eight-year-old and a five-year-old. You sure you want to do that now? You have a pension; you have health insurance."

I said, "Yes, absolutely. I believe in it so much that I'm willing to leave that behind and start owning my own practice because I need to be independent, so I can provide the best possible advice to people, and help them better than ever before." Her response was "Go for it."

So in 1999, I formed Fairway Financial—I like golf and thought the name had a nice ring to it. I concluded that seminars would be a great way to meet a lot of people in one room and give them my message, so I began doing seminars, and was one of the first ones to do them on Cape Cod.

The results were more than I could possibly imagine. For my very first seminar, 200 people signed up. I only had room for 75 people in the room! I panicked a little bit, but then I called the hotel, booked two more dates, and delivered my message.

Since then, I still do my retirement planning dinner seminars, mostly on Cape Cod and in Plymouth, Massachusetts, but now I also do radio shows and speak at local libraries, where I give talks mainly on Social Security and how to maximize benefits.

Here is a quiz I use at my workshops. How many of these can you answer?

How's Your Retirement IQ? Take the Quiz

1. If a beneficiary inherits an IRA from you, their taxes due will be?

    A. They will pay NO taxes.

    B. They will pay ordinary income taxes but only on the gains.

    C. All the money is subject to ordinary income taxes.

2. If your beneficiaries inherit a non-qualified annuity from you, what will they owe in taxes?

    A. Annuity funds will pass tax-free.

    B. They will pay long-term capital gains tax but only on the gains.

C. They will pay ordinary income taxes on all of it.

D. They will pay ordinary income taxes but only on the gains.

3. If Bob and Mary lose 30 percent in the stock market, how much do they need to gain to get back to where they were?

A. 30 percent

B. 35 percent

C. 43 percent

D. 53 percent

4. Bob and Mary each have Social Security. His is for $1,000, and hers for $500. On the death of the first spouse, the following is generally true.

A. The check for $500 will stop.

B. The check for $1,000 will stop.

C. The surviving spouse will receive $750.

D. There will be no change in income.

5. Bob and Mary have been married for 48 years. Bob has retired and has a pension of $2,000 a month and has chosen the most common pension option, leaving Mary with?

A. 100 percent of his pension.

B. 75 percent of his pension.

C. 50 percent of his pension.

D. Nothing but the keys to his car!

6. Now combine questions 5 and 6 and tell me how much annual income Mary would lose if she survives Bob?

A. $18,000

B. $12,000

C. $6,000

D. No loss of income

7. The current per person Federal Estate-Tax-Free limit is roughly?

A. $500,000

B. $1,000,000

C. $5,000,000

D. $11,200,000

8. True or false. A revocable living trust protects my estate from liability suits. T / F

How did you do? You'll find the answers at the back of this book.

Another reason I sat down and put together this book was that after 30 years of seeing depressions, recessions, bull markets, and bear markets, I've gained practical real-world knowledge first hand. I know how confusing this process gets, and I wanted to provide a resource that would lay out what the typical person goes through in the retirement income planning process and how to gather the appropriate information to make an intelligent decision.

Pre-planning for retirement is the optimal place to begin, but if you're already retired, then adjustments can be made. It's never too late to make a plan—a blueprint. We lay it out, make adjustments, act on it, and then monitor that blueprint every year to make sure that we keep you on track. I told you I like golf: My goal is to keep you on the fairway and out of the traps, then hopefully onto the green and into the cup.

Life throws us a lot of curves. We need to be able to deal with those and handle them appropriately with logic, not emotion. I want to help you handle them professionally so that you can have that retirement you want—travel, see your grandkids, and do what you want to do in your retirement years without worrying about outliving your money.

The Paradigm Shift

One of my biggest challenges is changing the mindset of people who have been accumulating assets in retirement accounts and are reaching that **critical stage**: the five years before retirement and the five years after retirement. You may still be thinking the same way as when you were 30, 40, or 50 years old. You're still in **accumulation mode**. But as you approach retirement age, you must understand you are about to shift into what I call the **decumulation mode**, or income mode. That involves this process of coordinating your Social Security, your pensions if you have them, and your retirement assets—your 401(k) 403(b), 457, TSA, TSP. All those plans need to be coordinated because they all fall under different rules.

There is a tremendous difference between the accumulation phase of your life and the income phase of your life. Like anything else in life, if you use your tools the wrong way, or if you use a tool for the wrong reason, you're not going to get the results you want. It's the same with the retirement income process.

When I speak with clients, I remind them about **why** we save for our retirement. It's not just to accumulate a pile of money. It's so we can use those savings in retirement to replace the income we were earning during our working years. Remember the key word is **income**.

And finally, I'm writing this because I'm living it now in my 50s. I'm taking the necessary steps to prepare for retirement, and I've had 30 years of doing this. I want to help you better understand your options and make intelligent, fact-based choices.

There's a lot of noise out there about what to do with your money. They all have their biases, as do I. But I am biased towards providing greater piece of mind for my clients by giving them the lifetime income they need and the opportunity to earn a competitive return **without** risking their money to market losses. So let's turn the page and begin your journey to gain greater peace of mind.

PART I

GATHERING THE PIECES (PRE-/POST-RETIREMENT)

Chapter 1

Setting the Table

You can set the table before or after you retire; the earlier, the better. If you are already retired, some pieces cannot be changed, like Social Security and pensions. But otherwise the process is similar.

To put together an effective retirement income plan and strategy, you first need to gather the pieces. It's like cooking. Before you can cook you've got to get all the ingredients in place. Then you follow the cookbook. You'll know what to add, and how to add it, and how to make it all just right. It's kind of the same with retirement income planning.

First you must understand what pieces you have and what's available to you. It doesn't matter whether you're 50, 55, 60 or 65. Everyone's number is going to be different. Personally, I don't believe in asking "what your number is" for retirement. We read about that and we see it a lot on TV, but there really is no one magic number for any one person. It only creates unrealistic expectations and it can serve to pigeonhole you. You start trying to compare yourself to a number or to someone else and that's dangerous. What you need to do is step back from that and see exactly where you are now. We'll compare where you are now to where you want to be in the future and then take steps to get you there. That is a more professional approach.

I gather facts, including your statements and documents. This determines your **three-legged stool of retirement**. When you retire, you need to have all three legs for your retirement to be stable; otherwise it's going to fall over.

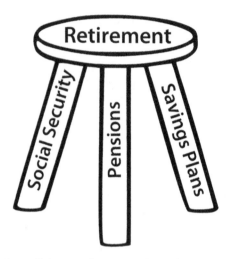

The first leg of the stool is your **Social Security**, which is a staple of your retirement. That's because it is a guaranteed source of income. It is designed to never run out. I know the Social Security system is under a lot of scrutiny and stress. It has been since the '80s and that won't change. And most likely it will never disappear.

The second leg of the stool, unfortunately, is disappearing: **pensions**. If you're fortunate enough to have a pension, and are not retired yet, we will need to take a close look at it to make sure that we maximize the plan. What I mean by that is we need to understand what the options are. We'll look more closely at those options in a later chapter.

The pension is very important, but unfortunately, it's becoming extinct, like the dinosaurs. Typically, the only folks who have pensions these days are government workers, state workers, and teachers.

The third leg of the stool is your **retirement savings plans**: IRAs, 401(k)s 403(b)s, 457s, TSAs, TSPs—basically all these government-offered programs that started to take effect back in the late '70s.

Now, when we look at that stool, there are only two legs that are guaranteed for life: the pension and Social Security. The danger today—the biggest threat to your retirement—is that 401(k) plans, 403(b) plans, and IRAs are **not guaranteed** to provide a lifetime income. If you don't have a pension plan and treat your 401(k) and 403(b) like one, you may miscalculate, and you may run out of money. You could be stuck at age 75 or 78 with no other income than Social Security. That is obviously a situation that you want to avoid at all costs. That's one of the biggest threats that I see out there: the mismanagement of retirement assets to produce income. These are very important pieces of the puzzle, but financial assets aren't the only consideration.

Another consideration is health insurance. Where is your medical insurance going to come from, and how will it be funded? Also, we must address the real possibility that you may suffer a long-term illness and be placed in a nursing home. According to the National Clearinghouse for Long-Term Care Information, a person's risk of needing long-term care services in their lifetime is 1 out of 2; that's a 50 percent risk. As age increases, so does the likelihood of needing long-term care; 70 percent of people over the age of 65 will require some type of long-term care services during their lifetime.[1] Whether you have a plan for that or not, we must understand and include it in your retirement income planning.

Lastly, you need to consider your own health. If you're 60 or 65 years old and you're in great health, and if you have good family history, then there's a real possibility you're going to need income for 25 or 30 years.

However, if your health is not so good, then what? It may determine when we take Social Security, and what pension option to elect.

Seem daunting? Yes, but that's why there are professionals like myself with years of experience who have helped hundreds of individuals and couples do this. I understand the process. When you visit me with your statements, goals, and dreams, I have the tools and the techniques that enable us—together—to design a well-thought-out retirement plan. I want to be your financial quarterback.

I always get excited about the process. Where are you going to travel? Will you take a hobby that you did and make it into maybe some fun part-time income? Are your kids and grandkids close? Do you have a lot of friends? Do you take trips? Are you a golfer or a fisherman? All these dreams and goals are why we work. It's what keeps us going, right? It's what motivates us to get out of bed and work 9-to-5? In the end, we want to do the things that we like to do the most.

Once we have all the pieces laid out, the key is to put them together wisely in what I call my buckets of wealth, so that we can guarantee the lifetime income that you need and deserve.

The Critical Years

The five years immediately preceding your retirement and the five years right after you retire are what I call the **critical years**. The years before you retire are your set-up years, when you're looking at your assets and making some subtle changes, knowing that you now have less time to accumulate. You might be backing off some of your aggressive stances and setting them up for the distribution phase. You're probably looking at your 401(k)s and your IRAs differently than you did when you were 30 or 40 years old.

This is where you start to gather the pieces together. You want to make sure your Social Security statements are accurate, so that your benefits are computed correctly. If you have a pension, you are starting to look at the numbers more closely. This is the pre-planning stage, and it's essential.

Similar to the pre-planning that takes place during the five years before retirement, the first five years after retirement are just as important because that's when, despite all your best efforts, situations arise that you may not have accounted for correctly; expenses may be higher, the market may have drastically changed or health issues may occur. So once again it's important to monitor and review.

It's like becoming a parent. You can plan all you want, but the reality is never quite the same. When you have kids, there are so many contingencies. So many things come up that you thought you had planned for. As a parent myself, I get it now, in a way I didn't then. My son just got engaged and whenever he talks about family, my wife and I just look at each other with a "Yeah, been there, done that," grin on our faces, thinking, "Just you wait."

Buckets of Wealth

People love to talk about creating **Buckets of Wealth**, and it's a lot of fun to help folks build them, because for the most part, we all are visual learners. And to be able to see your money at work in a logical laid out manner helps to create greater financial confidence.

I do this at my workshops. If you have ever attended one of my workshops, you'll know what I mean. I pull out actual buckets and I pull out bags of money—pennies, nickels, dimes, and quarters. I pour the money into these buckets and I talk about the **Now bucket,** which provides our current income, which for pre-retirees is our earnings, and for retirees consists mostly of Social Security, pensions, and IRA distributions. Next is the **Later/fun bucket,** which we ultimately want to use to replace the now bucket for those of us still working and supplement our income for retirees as an inflation hedge. It is also our fun and travel bucket, so most folks want to fill that to the very top. The third is the **Never/emergency bucket,** which we use for emergencies only, or as a legacy transfer to our spouse and/or children. Since we never plan on using it, we should never have to pay taxes on it, and I can show you how. The fourth is the **Tax bucket,** which needs to be controlled. Our goal is to pour more of the money into the Now and Later/fun buckets, and less into the Tax bucket. There are ways to balance that, and we'll talk about balance in a later chapter.

Now that we have set the table, let's take a closer look at the individual pieces and how they fit into the puzzle.

Chapter 2

Social Security and Pensions

SOCIAL SECURITY AND PENSIONS are the foundation of your retirement plan because they represent guaranteed lifetime income, with survivor options if elected. For most of us, they will represent most of our income.

One, pensions, are a dying breed. The other, Social Security, is also in danger but can and most likely will be saved.

Social Security

Social Security, as you probably know, was created in 1935 by President Franklin Roosevelt in response to the Great Depression. It was a way to calm the public and to reassure the public that all would be good, and we were going to have a bright future.

It was the first socialized program in the country and was designed with the right goal in mind: to protect the American public and give us a sense of security.

But just as we are living longer today, placing a lot more stress on our retirement portfolio to last longer, the Social Security system is paying out more checks than the current workers can support. That is why as of the writing of this book, Social Security is supposedly going to be bankrupt in 2034. However, Social Security is an extremely important benefit. In fact, Social Security is the major source of income for most of the elderly. Among elderly Social Security beneficiaries, 50 percent of married couples and 71 percent of unmarried persons receive half or more of their income from Social Security.[2] So I am confident that it will be here for a very long time into the future. That's why it's so important to make a wise decision about how to take your Social Security check.

Here's the challenge, and it's something most people don't realize: <u>There are over 500 different claiming options that you can elect regarding your Social Security.</u> And one of the biggest challenges is that the law does not allow the Social Security Administration to give advice. They are only allowed to give numbers. Because of that, people often just equate Social Security with retiring.

They'll say, "I'm going to retire at 65 or 66 and I'm going to take my Social Security. End of discussion." For my generation, for my birthday, my full retirement is 67. I firmly believe that the government will continue to push the age up to age 70.

To find out about your benefits, visit the Social Security Administration website, www.ssa.gov. Set up an account online and monitor it to make sure that your quarterly hours and your wages are reported properly. If you don't monitor it, and you find out when get your check that it's been changed, it's too late. You can't go back and change it.

When Do I Take Social Security?

This is the critical question everyone needs to answer, and unfortunately many people make a mistake with it. Most people assume that that they should take their Social Security at full retirement age and defer drawing on their IRA and their 401(k). But that can be a major mistake. Why? Because current law says that between your full retirement age and age 70, your Social Security benefits will be guaranteed to increase by eight percent.

I doubt that you can say the same for your retirement plan. Unfortunately, many people don't get very good advice on this. Therefore, you need to have all the facts to make an informed decision.

You need good advice. Most of us don't know what we don't know. And we also don't know what to ask. That's where I come in. I do know what to ask. I've gotten on the phone with Social Security and my clients and we get the right answers.

We need to figure out all your benefits. It's very easy to do online. You'll have all your statements, so we'll know what you would receive at age 62; we'll know your full retirement age—whether it is 66 or 67 or somewhere in between—and we'll know what you would receive if you defer to age 70, which is the maximum amount your Social Security will accrue to. Also, if you plan on taking Social Security at 62 and you continue to work, you may not be eligible to receive all your benefits. You read that correctly! For 2018, that number is $17,040. Workers who earn more than this will have $1 in benefits withheld for every $2 in earned income over the limit. For those turning 66 in 2018, the earnings limit is $45,360. Their payment reduction will also decline by $1 for every $3 above the earnings limit. There is NO income limit over full retirement age.

If you're still working and you don't need the money, then most likely you should defer your Social Security until a later age, with 70 being the maximum.

The numbers are a big factor in your decision-making, but they're not the only factor you need to consider. Your health also has bearing. That's because Social Security is an all-encompassing plan. It's a pension plan with a survivor benefit, which is another form of life insurance. That means we must look not only at what the check brings while we're living, but what the survivor will receive after the death of a spouse.

It's very important to figure that out and I'll help you to do that. If your health is not good, it may make sense to take your Social Security check early. If you have a spouse, it's important to understand what the spousal benefits are. If you were born on or before January 1, 1954, you have options as a spouse to restrict off your spouse's Social Security check and take half of their check, but you must meet certain criteria.

If you were born before that date, you've got to wait to your full retirement and then you may restrict off your spouse and take half of that check, especially if that check exceeds your own check. Let's say that half of your spouse's check exceeds your benefit. You would take that check until maybe at some point your deferred check—your own Social Security check—starts to build up so that at age say 69 or 70, if your own personal check exceeds your spouse's you can then switch. That's a little something most people aren't aware of, and it could put hundreds and hundreds of dollars a month in your pocket. That law is still in effect.

A Social Security story: John and Carol

Sometimes the best way to explain these concepts is with a real-life example. Let me tell you about John and Carol, a nice couple who came to see me a while ago.

I met them through one of the Social Security workshops that I do at a public library. John was 66 and eligible for full retirement. Carol was 64. They both had Social Security; John also had a small pension and some 401(k)s and such. John was thinking about taking his Social Security, but he did have other sources of monies that he could use. He basically said, "I think I want to take it now." And I said, "Well, that's fine. Let's get the numbers."

We worked through the process of determining what his income would be now versus what it would be if he waited four years, until he turns 70. John learned that by waiting four years, his Social Security check would be 32 percent higher. This was important for both John and Carol; remember that with Social Security the surviving spouse receives the higher of the two checks.

In this case, John's initial check was just slightly higher than Carol's, but because he had put in so many years and Carol had already stopped working, his check was going to be a lot bigger.

We decided to defer John's Social Security and then have him live off his other assets, which were some brokerage accounts and some monies in the bank. Certainly, none of those were guaranteeing eight percent for the four years. He needed about $20,000–25,000 a year. He had about $100,000 in the brokerage account and another $25,000 in the bank. We just took from a little bit over those four years, and lo and behold—at age 70 years old John's check is going to be 32 percent higher and the survivor check is going to be that much higher as well.

By just running the numbers I was able to help John and Carol make a comfortable decision. They felt good about it and they told me, "We're so happy we took the time to meet you, Steve." They made an informed decision.

Remember, the Social Security Administration cannot, by law, give advice. They can only give you your numbers. That's why it's a great idea to get together just to do a Social Security review.

The Bottom Line on Social Security

To sum up, Social Security is a program that offers hundreds of different claiming strategies. You must gather your numbers, then sit down with every other piece of information that you have on your other retirement assets to coordinate a strategy that will determine whether you should take Social Security now and defer the IRAs or defer Social Security until 70 and take the IRAs now. To make a wise decision, you need to look at all the facts, and run all the numbers.

You should not make a Social Security claiming decision on its own merits. You need to factor it in with everything else: your health, your pensions, and your other assets. If you don't do that, you could be making a mistake that could literally cost you hundreds of thousands of dollars.

Pensions (The ABCs of Income Options)

Pensions are another form of lifetime income: guaranteed checks. Pensions are called defined benefit plans, and again, there are options to consider in how you take them. Generally speaking there are three options, A, B, and C. The first option pays the worker only and disinherits the spouse. The other two have survivor options.

Let's use an example based on a typical pension—based on average earnings and years of service—that produces $60,000 a year for life for you only as the worker. This represents Option A. If you were to die in one year or the next day, then it's gone. The pension dies with you. That $60,000 would be gone forever. So if you have a spouse, you need to examine the survivor benefit options. The next benefit, Option B, is typically called "joint and one-half," which means that you would both get the same check while living and on the death of one spouse, the survivor would get half. Typically, it might cost you 10 percent, or in our example $6,000, for that option. You as the employee would get $54,000 a year while you are both living. At the death of the employee, the survivor would get half, or $27,000. Joint with 50 percent is the most popular pension option in the country.

You might also have an Option C, commonly called "joint and two-thirds." Under that option the survivor would receive two-thirds of the check instead of half. But it's going to cost a little bit more. So instead of charging $6,000, the company charges $12,000. The pension goes from $60,000 to $48,000, but then the survivor gets two-thirds of that check, or $32,000.

Essentially, what you're doing is buying life insurance. So the real decision is whether to buy it from your former employer, or thru a private insurance company. The answer in most questions depends on your health. If you're in decent health, you might want to consider a private life insurance company. But to do that right, you need to run the numbers. Let's say you're going to do the Option B, as we described above. You're going to give up $6,000 a year to provide an annual $27,000 survivor benefit. To determine how much of a lump sum you would need to provide $27,000 a year for your spouse's lifetime, we run an illustration with some conservative return assumptions.

Let's say that number is $500,000. For a person at age 64, with $6,000 a year, that will buy just about $500,000 of private life insurance. If the numbers show that it's better to do it privately then you do it. If the numbers show it's not better, then you don't do it. In the case above it makes sense to buy the life insurance privately.

I've seen too many insurance agents out there just take the difference in the pension, plug in a number and say, "Oh, it's $300,000; that's plenty of money. It'll last forever." But certainly $300,000 will not replace $27,000 forever. I've seen that mistake made too many times by unknowledgeable advisors.

A pension story: Mike and Joan

Mike's story demonstrates why it's so important to consider your pension options carefully. Mike worked for a municipality in the state of Massachusetts. He attended one of my dinner seminars on retirement planning, and afterward he called and made an appointment to come into my office with his wife Joan. The three of us sat down and Mike said, "Steve, I'm retiring in six months." He said, "Here are all my numbers; let's put all the pieces of the puzzle together." Mike was only 61. We knew what his Social Security was, and we knew that he was going to defer it for four years to at least age 66; we were all pretty comfortable with that.

Mike was more concerned about his pension. He had heard some water cooler talk at work that some people were taking the B and C options through their employer, but other people were buying private life insurance. He really wasn't sure what to do.

We sat down and worked through his pension numbers. He was in great health. If he took his Option B—joint and one-half—it would have cost him a little over $10,000 reduction in his check to do so. That would provide half for Joan in the event of his death.

Using that information, I was able to determine that we would need roughly $475,000 in life insurance. Because Mike was so healthy, we were able, for $10,000, to buy more than that. We ended up closer to $600,000 tax-free. Imagine how elated he was to learn that we could not only provide a higher amount tax-free but also give him the opportunity, because he now owned this privately, to get his money back. Mike would put in $10,000 of premiums for 20 years. After those 20 years, if his wife predeceased him, the insurance company would write him a check for all those premiums, totaling $200,000. They would write a check back to him tax-free because it was a return of his money.

He loved that idea. I told him, "That's what you call the power of leverage." We wrote the policy, he funded the policy, and he's very happy with the decision. He even referred a few co-workers to me.

This was just a first step for Mike and Joan. We're going to be meeting again to discuss the other elements of their retirement income plan, to utilize one of my "secret sauces" of retirement income planning. I'll tell you more about those in a later chapter.

The Bottom Line on Pensions

To summarize on pensions, it's about examining your options, looking at the differences among the A, B and C plans. Then it's determining whether you want to add a survivor option and if so, whether it would be better to do that privately or to do it with your employer.

There can be another benefit of doing it privately. There are some insurance products out there that will guarantee a return of your money after so many years. So, think about this. If you're torn between the two, and it's a close decision, what if a company was willing for $8,000 to give you, say $475,000? The computer said you needed $500,000, but in 20 years, you could get back all the money that you put in, if you wanted. It's something to consider.

In 20 years, that's $160,000 of your own money back. Why would you consider doing that? Well, let's say you both make it to 20 years. Maybe you have five, six, seven years to go. You don't need the big pile anymore. And what if your spouse predeceases you and you no longer need that life insurance? In that case, in 20 years you're going to get all your money back, guaranteed in writing. That's a pretty good deal, so you should think about that.

As I said earlier, the reason I wrote this book is to offer education. Take advantage of that. Get the facts. Get the knowledge. Don't settle for hearsay or noise. Get the actual numbers that you can understand so that you can make an intelligent decision.

Social Security and pensions are both forms of guaranteed checks. They provide lifetime income and they each have different claiming options. You need to examine those options before you retire, and you need to thoroughly understand how best to integrate them with your other assets so that you're able to make the right decision. That informed decision will not only benefit you and your spouse now, but your children and grandchildren later in the form of a tax-free legacy plan.

Chapter 3

Retirement Savings Accounts

Now we get into that alphabet soup of retirement planning—the 401(k)s, 403(b)s, 457s and IRAs. Most of us have our wealth in these plans and are going to rely on them more heavily than ever before, especially as pensions disappear completely. Remember our three-legged stool? As we lose that guaranteed pension leg, we must be more concerned about making sure that the money we've saved in our own plans will be guaranteed to provide us with a lifetime check. And because we are living longer, we are placing more stress on our retirement portfolios to produce that outcome.

This is the biggest financial challenge we face at retirement. But this is also where we have the most control and flexibility. So, as we talk about how to manage that, let me start by telling you about the four types of money that are available to help set the stage.

The Four Types of Money

Free Money
We all like free, right? Free money comes from maybe hitting a lottery, or receiving an inheritance, or most commonly, a 401(k) or a 403(b) match. If you are working for an employer, and you have one of those plans, and they offer a match—say they will match 100 percent up to three percent, or up to six percent—that money is free money. They are matching your payroll deduction contribution

dollar for dollar, so you're getting 100 percent return on your money. That's free money.

Tax-Free Money

If you can't get free money, the next best thing is tax-free. There are several categories of tax-free money. A Roth IRA, or even a Roth 401(k) or Roth 403(b), is generally tax-free money. All the money grows tax-free, not deferred, but FREE. Municipal bonds can also be tax-free, if you live in the state in which you purchase that bond. And another category of tax-free money that often gets overlooked, perhaps more so than any other asset: Cash value life insurance. That's right; If you own cash value life insurance, it can fall into the tax-free category of money.

Tax-Deferred Money

This is where we hold most of our wealth, because the tax-deferred category is made up of IRAs, 401(k)s, 403(b)s, 457 plans, and TSAs (Tax Sheltered Annuities).

This is by far the largest category of wealth in the country. It's also the one that is going to experience the most change, as I alluded to earlier. The first of the baby boomers hit age 70 in 2016. And as we age, we're going to see the biggest transfer of wealth from the market to our pockets in history through force-outs or Required Minimum Distributions (RMDs). This also represents the largest planning opportunity for those pre- and post-retirees who are educated. More on this in a moment.

Taxable Money

The fourth type of money is taxable accounts. This will consist of bank savings accounts, checking accounts, and brokerage accounts—pretty much everything else not listed in the first three categories.

Why is it so important to understand these categories? Because when it comes to retirement planning you want to take advantage of the best category first; free money, followed by tax-free, followed by tax-deferred. The biggest mistake I've seen the baby boomer generation make is that we have most of our money in category three and have virtually skipped category two. This is mostly because Roth IRAs are a relatively new invention; they came out roughly in the late '90s. And most people have become used to taking the deduction now.

The Seed and the Harvest (Pay me now, or pay me later)

Back in the late '70s and '80s, there was a TV commercial from an oil filter company. It went something like this: You can pay me now or you can pay me later. What they meant by that was if you spent a little to do your normal maintenance and get an oil change every 3,000 to 4,000 miles, it would save you a fortune down the road. Without the right maintenance on your car, your engine could overheat, and it would cost you more money than it would have ever cost you to do the maintenance. The same holds true with retirement planning.

Here's another analogy. A farmer buys seed to plant so that at the end of the season he can harvest his crop. When a farmer buys his seed, it's a small amount of seed that will be planted to produce hopefully a very large harvest. As the farmer, would you rather pay taxes on the seed, which is a smaller investment, or would you rather pay taxes on the harvest, which if we do it right is a much larger pile? The answer, of course, is that you would rather pay taxes on the seed, because it's a smaller amount.

Now think of that logic in terms of investments that you hold. A Roth account holder is somebody who is willing to pay taxes now—to pay taxes on that seed—so that in the future all the money that's grown is tax-free. If you have monies in those tax-deferred accounts, which most of us do, you have chosen to pay taxes later. Before you get nervous and think, "Oh my goodness, I made a big mistake," understand that you are in the same boat as most Americans. And you didn't necessarily make a mistake, because if you have some time prior to age 70 and a half—and even beyond that in some cases—we can address the situation. Also, even if you are already retired, you have some amazing planning opportunities. Let's examine a typical company match situation, and how we can be proactive.

Money Migration: How Free can stay Free.

Let's look again at the four categories of money and see what happens for a typical employee with a pre-tax 401(k) match. Suppose you have your money matched at three percent. Remember that match falls into category one; it's free money. But if you leave it in there and allow it to accumulate, it accumulates in category three. The accumulation is tax-deferred.

If you had a match on a Roth 401(k), your match is in category one, which is free money. But in a Roth 401(k) it would drop to category two, not category three, and the growth would be tax-free. It's important to understand where your money is held and how it's accountable in the future in terms of tax planning.

Remember, we'd rather pay taxes on the seed than on the harvest, and it's never too late to make some changes to our situation, through what is called a Roth conversion.

To Roth or not to Roth? It's not what you earn, it's what you keep.

That is the question. The answer is based mainly upon your tax situation. And right now taxes, believe it or not, are on sale in America. Historically we are in a very low tax environment, and the new tax bill just lowered it again for most Americans. I know you might be saying to yourself, "Steve, you're crazy. I'm paying a lot of taxes." If you're working and are making a high salary, that could be true. You may think you're paying a lot of taxes. But if you look at your effective tax yield after your deductions in many cases you're going to be quite surprised to see that compared to the past you are in a lower tax bracket.

Here's a question: If you were able to pay a one-time tax of 15 to 20 percent, and then never ever have to pay taxes again on that money, would you do it? If the answer is yes, then you should strongly consider doing what is called a **Roth conversion**. That means moving some of your tax-deferred assets, which are in category three, over into category two, and paying the one-time tax now. By doing so, in the future you will control your taxable situation, and control your distributions, because once you move your money to category two the government no longer requires you to take a minimum distribution at 70 and a half. In other words, you now have complete control of your retirement plan.

You need to sit down with a professional like myself who's been doing this for a long time, who understands the right questions to ask. And you need to work in harmony with your CPA.

You want to keep as much control as possible over your retirement assets. This is not just a pile of money. It's your future income, and you need to focus on what that pile of money can produce, for you and your spouse for the remainder of your lives.

You need to start looking at these assets differently, and you need to approach them differently, so that we can put this piece together with your Social Security and your pension, if you have one, as part of a coordinated strategy. It's all about putting the pieces together. And your retirement savings are the most important piece, because they offer you the most flexibility, the most control, and the greatest number of options.

Another decision is whether or not to roll over your 401(k) plan into your own personal IRA plan, or leave it as is.

Speaking of rollovers: Charlie's story

Charlie came to me wondering about his retirement options. He was 62 years old and he was a widower. Charlie had three IRAs, two 401(k)s, and a Roth IRA. His biggest question was whether he should leave the 401(k)s at his former employer or roll it over to his own IRA. He had no pension and was currently taking income as needed. But his ultimate goal was to create a lifetime guaranteed income check for him and his wife. He came into my office with all his paperwork and we had a nice meeting. We talked about utilizing annuity options to guarantee the future paycheck he was looking for. Then we looked at whether he should do a rollover.

After making some phone calls, we learned that Charlie's 401(k) administrator did have some high fees. His fund choices weren't bad, but he could duplicate them on the outside for slightly less money. Charlie also learned that 401(k)s have their own set of rules when you're retired. Because it's an employer-sponsored plan, when you reach age 70 and a half, each plan is responsible for doing its own RMD. In this case, he had two 401(k)s, and three IRAs. He was going to end up having multiple distributions, and after talking about the pros and cons, we decided to combine and rollover his 401(k)s into an IRA indexed annuity. This would allow him to capture indexed gains but with no direct downside risk. But more importantly, eight years from now, we would be able to turn on a guaranteed income check for him and his wife to supplement his Social Security. More on this type of annuity later in the book. The rollover was simple to do, and it would allow him to aggregate his IRAs and take distributions from one account.

That one rollover we did would, in eight years, guarantee Charlie an income check for life. And that one income check would also satisfy the IRA rules for minimum distribution on all his accounts. Charlie loved that. This was an example of a rollover that made perfect sense: We were able to lower Charlie's expenses, gain more control over his options, manage his direct downside market exposure, and simplify the process.

So when considering a rollover, some of the key factors are; risk, fees, control, income needs, and flexibility.

The IRA Rescue Plan

As I described above, you can do a Roth conversion and rescue that money from future taxes. But what if you have already retired, and you've already reached age 70 and a half? Suppose you've already taken your RMDs, but you really don't need that income.

That's a nice position to be in. If you have a strong pension, good Social Security benefits, and low debt, maybe you are one of those folks who are fortunate enough not to need your RMDs. The question becomes how to take that money. Most people take the money and stick it right in the bank. They'll pay the tax, and they'll put the rest in the bank.

Here's another possibility, one that I've shared with my clients over the years, with great results. What if I could take that RMD, after tax, and instead of putting it into your bank, at one or two per cent, we put it into my "bank"? In return, we could produce a stepped-up **tax-free** benefit at death that would essentially replace the entire IRA tax-free.

I call this my "guilt-free" living plan. You can take the RMDs and do that, then spend the rest of that IRA money down to zero, and still, at your death, be able to pass all that money tax-free to either your spouse or your children. It uses leverage of the money, and it's very easily transferrable. If you are interested in pursuing this, give my office a call. We can design an IRA rescue plan specifically for you, your age, and your needs.

IRA rescue: Bob and Pat's story

Bob and Pat have been clients of mine for some time. Because they are both over 70, they have been taking their RMDs; the law requires that.

I gave them a call to schedule our annual review and Bob said, "You know, Steve, you've done such a good job planning for us that our pension, Social Security and annuity are providing us with enough income. We really don't need the RMDs. It's really such a shame that we have to take them, pay the taxes, and then deposit them in the bank."

I asked him about his goal for that money. He said, "I don't know. I think we're just going to leave it there, let it accumulate, and eventually at death we're going to leave it to our kids." I replied, "How about this? What if I can take those RMDs and leverage them to replace your IRA tax-free for pennies on the dollar?" Of course, he was very interested.

We did it using life insurance. Bob's RMD was $8,000. Based on his age and his health, we were able to secure a policy for $175,000 tax-free with a deposit of $8,000 every year. That is just incredible for someone who is in their 70s to be able to do that. Bob was thrilled to be able to take that money from his IRA and to move it, after tax, into a vehicle that would be tax-free for his spouse, or if she didn't need it, their kids. Bob was thrilled to "rescue" his IRA.

Now that we have rescued it, Bob says, "You know, maybe I will take some of that IRA principal after all and start taking extra vacations, knowing that I'm replacing it tax-free." Both Bob and his wife Pat are extremely happy with their decision. I call that guilt-free living with tax-free planning.

Retirement Insurance

We all have insurance on our homes and cars. Most of us have life insurance. We understand that need. But do we have **retirement insurance**? In other words, are your retirement assets—that big pile of money you saved—insured? Is it insured in case the market goes down? Is it insured to provide a guaranteed income for life?

Think about that for a moment. As we look at all the reasons why we have insurance, doesn't it make sense to insure the most valuable asset you have; your retirement savings? I can show you how to guarantee not only a check for you and your spouse, but still have the opportunity to grow, without any direct downside market risk. It's a way to earn interest credits based on the movement of a market index while avoiding direct downside market risk. More on this strategy for building and distributing wealth with greater peace of mind later in this book.

Chapter 4

Medical Care and Long-Term Care

THERE ARE TWO distinct categories here. The first is **short-term acute care**. That includes your hospital stays, your prescriptions, your doctor visits, and all those short-term care needs—also known as health insurance.

Anything longer than that—typically 100 days or more—is called **chronic or long-term care**. That could involve an extended stay in a hospital, but most of the time long-term care encompasses four levels of care. These are nursing home care, adult daycare, assisted living care, and home health care.

Health Insurance

Some folks are fortunate enough to be able to take their medical insurance with them when they retire, depending on what age they are. If you are in that situation, and if you're under 65, then that health insurance will become your primary insurance. You may read about people who don't get paid a lot in wages, but their benefits packages are excellent. Some folks will forego higher pay for the benefits and having health insurance paid for or partially paid for is a huge benefit.

When you reach age 65, then you are eligible for Medicare. Medicare Part A, hospital coverage, becomes your primary care and that's free. Medicare Part B is your doctor visits and your prescriptions, which you pay for.

If you don't have any other medical insurance, you can take your Medicare A and B, and then buy what is called a **med supplement plan.**

The Medicare supplement plan is exactly that. It will pick up your co-pays for your hospital care, your doctor visits, and of course your prescriptions.

If you're healthy, then you will want to buy a supplemental policy that has fewer prescription drug benefits, which will save you money. If you are currently taking prescription medications, then you need to look at a plan that will cover prescriptions.

So, as far as medical insurance goes, it's typically a combination of Medicare and your own private health insurance, or If you don't have private health insurance, Medicare, and a good supplemental plan.

Unfortunately, health insurance does not cover long-term care. It only covers acute, short-term care: hospital stays, operations, doctor visits, prescriptions, and the like. It will generally not cover nursing home stays that exceed 100 days, home health care, or assisted living.

Some of you reading this book may be veterans, and the VA has some very limited coverage. Of course, they have facilities that will provide some level of care. But don't make the mistake of thinking that because you're a veteran that you're completely covered because unfortunately, you're not.

Long-term Care

Long-term care is the gorilla in the room. We all know about it, and none of us want to talk about it. When I talk about it in my seminars, I always ask, "How many people in this room know somebody who's been in a nursing home or needed home health care?" Inevitably, 70–80 percent of those in the room raise their hands.

This is a major problem in our country and a major threat to one's financial security and peace of mind. Don't think that because you're fine and you're healthy now, that you're never going to need care. Remember, Noah didn't build the ark after it rained!

How do we deal with this epidemic? The numbers say that married couples age 65 will have a 40 percent chance of needing some form of long-term care at some point in their lives. That's a staggering number. Also, statistics say that the average couple will spend over $250,000 on medical care during their retirement years. This is something we need to address, and we shouldn't just ignore it.

Yes, we do come full circle in life. We are brought into this world fully dependent on people, and in many cases, we end up leaving this world dependent on people. In my 30 years of experience, I have seen a lot of that. I've dealt with people who were perfectly healthy one day, had a stroke the next day, and then were in a nursing home for five months. I have seen nursing homes wipe out entire estates.

From what I've learned in my 30 plus years in the business, there are only three ways we can address this problem.

Self-Insurance

That is basically to say, "Steve, I know the problem. I understand the problem but I'm just going to try to have some money set aside to take care of it. If I don't have enough money set aside, then I'm going to go on Medicaid," which is a form of welfare.

Most married couples can keep about $125,000 of liquid assets. As you plan for this you need to work with an elder law attorney, an attorney who specializes in this area.

An attorney is going to talk about trusts and Medicaid planning but understand that Medicaid is welfare. If you chose to go that route, you become a ward of the state, and they will determine where to place you for care; it's no longer up to you. And some states have the right to estate recovery, which means they may place a lien on your home after you die to recover monies used to pay for your care.

Traditional Long-Term Care Insurance

Long-term care insurance is a good alternative, because you are ceding the risk. You are getting rid of an unknown risk with a known premium. Today's policies typically pay for all levels of care but bear in mind that insurance companies have guessed wrong when it comes to underwriting these policies. I have seen large premium increases from certain insurance carriers. I'm not saying it's not the right way to go, but if you have the money and you're able to pay for a long-term care policy and premium, sometimes it's better to pay a stated amount annually, with maybe a 10 to 15 percent increase in the future and eliminate a risk that could literally cost hundreds and hundreds of thousands of dollars.

In my state of Massachusetts, the average cost of nursing home care is about $100,000. Wherever you live, make no mistake, it's an extremely expensive proposition.

Long-term care: Jim and Claire's story

Jim and Claire have been great clients of mine for over 17 years. When I met them, they had just turned 60. They retired as teachers from Connecticut and moved up here to Massachusetts. We put a couple of retirement pieces in place and were watching that plan come to fruition. The one open piece was the long-term care question.

After going over their options, we ended up putting together a traditional long-term care plan that would provide all levels of care at home or in a nursing home. They decided it made more sense to give up roughly $7,500 a year than to take the chance of giving up not only hundreds of thousands of dollars but also loss of control over where their care would be.

There's an epilogue to this story. A year ago, Jim was in perfectly good health. He was out walking one day, had a mini-stroke, collapsed, and needed to be in a nursing home for three or four months. Their policy paid for that stay. Jim and Claire were so happy that they had made that policy decision, because that short-term stay alone would have been about $50,000. In this case, the long-term care policy really paid dividends for them.

Leverage: Linked-Benefit Plans

Long-term care insurance is used by millions of people across the country. Here's the dilemma with that: It can be expensive. The insurance company has a right to raise the premium, and from a health standpoint, you may not qualify. You might consider another option, which is to use leverage. I'm a big fan of leverage. We talked about leverage in the previous chapter, where I described the IRA rescue plan. In this case, believe it or not, you can use a special form of life insurance, called a **linked-benefit plan**, to leverage your rainy-day fund. Let's say you have $75,000 to $100,000 in the bank, that you just kind of want there for emergencies. There's not a lot of leverage there. You've got $100,000 that's sitting in the bank at maybe one percent. Not a very productive bucket. But you like the liquidity it provides.

So how about this option? Let's create a leveraged bucket that addresses three scenarios: one, that you live a long healthy life; two, that you may die before your life expectancy; or three, that you may become disabled, and need some form of long-term care. Under the first scenario, living a healthy life, this money will just sit in an account and grow tax sheltered. It's not going to earn a lot of money, but neither is your bank, and you're going to have access to it, just like your savings account provides.

In the second scenario, if you die before your life expectancy, your new bucket will be stepped up from the original $100,000, and it will be tax-free to your beneficiaries. There's a tremendous use of a leverage to create this bucket that you may not need, and pass it on tax-free, at a higher amount.

Then there's the third scenario: What if you become disabled and need long-term care? In that case, this same bucket will step up again, and be able to provide a large, tax-free monthly benefit to cover your long-term care needs. It will cover them at your home, a nursing home, or an assisted living facility.

This option is gaining a lot of popularity, because it requires only one premium and it creates three potential checks: a check while you're living, a check when you pass away, and a check if you get sick and need long-term care. These plans can be customized for couples or for individuals, and they are gaining tremendous popularity. The underwriting on these products is not as stringent as the traditional long-term care plans. I highly recommend that when you're going through your process of retirement planning, and you get to the medical and long-term care considerations, run the numbers on this. I will go into greater detail about this product in my essential tools section, but for now, let me give you a real-life example.

Speaking of leverage: Tom and Sue's story

Let's look at an example of using leverage. Tom and Sue were in their early 60s and already had traditional long-term care insurance, which provided about $6000 a month in today's dollars. So we decided to look at what's new out there in the marketplace. After doing an assessment on their assets, I was able to describe an opportunity where we would take $100,000 each from their savings account and put it into this linked-benefit product. While living, it would be a savings account earning about 1-2 percent a year like their bank. When they died, it would step up to about $120,000 tax-free. But if either were to become disabled, it would pay the equivalent of about $7000 a month for five years. That was just incredible leverage.

At age 80, because we added an inflation rider, the long-term care payments would be close to $500,000—talk about leverage. Tom and Sue were thrilled about it. They had never heard of this before until now. They were writing a check they knew they would get back. If they lived, they had a guaranteed return of premium. If they ever changed their minds, they would get all their money back. When they died, there would be a tax-free death benefit paid to the beneficiary. And if they needed long-term care, it would pay upwards of half a million dollars. How could they go wrong with that?

As I said earlier, the purpose of my book is to educate people on their choices at retirement so that they can make intelligent, well-informed decisions. That's what I did here, and I'll bet that many of you reading this chapter right now probably are saying to yourself, "I've never even heard about this." Well, now you have to act and give us a call.

Chapter 5

Taxes, Taxes, and More Taxes

WE'VE REACHED THE POINT in this book where we need to discuss the inevitable: taxes. We all know that taxes are not going to go away. You know the old saying: The only two things that are certain in life are death and taxes.

First, let's be clear that we have no control over the tax brackets and the tax rates that the government establishes for us. However, we do have control over some of our assets to determine our own situation in terms of our tax bracket and tax liability.

Remember, as I said earlier, retirement planning is the process of examining how all the pieces fit together and what the tax implications are.

When you look at each of the pieces, you need to ask three questions:

1. How much income is this piece going to produce?
2. For how long is it going to produce that income?
3. What are the tax ramifications for that income?

The answers to these questions will vary with time and your retirement age. If you decide you want to retire at age 62, the answers will be different from those for age 65 or 66 or 70. Every time you set a new goal or age for your retirement, you need to ask these questions. How much income am I going to get? How long is it going to last? And what are the tax implications?

I believe that 50–60 percent of the retirement planning process involves the tax implications. It's that important. Earlier in this book we talked about Roth conversions. That can give you some tax control. Can you imagine being in a situation where you pay a one-time tax of 15–20 percent on your money, and then you never ever have to pay taxes again on that money?

Talk about tax control. With a Roth you pay no taxes going forward. You have no minimum distribution requirements at age 70 and a half, and when you do take that income, it doesn't count against the Social Security provisional tax.

Most people don't realize that the government comes up with its own provisional income tax to determine how Social Security gets taxed. Your taxable sources of income become a determining factor on how much of your Social Security check gets taxed.

That's why it's so important to go through this planning process and look at your tax situation. I've been able to help some couples put themselves in the zero percent tax bracket for the remainder of their lives. Of course, I can't control whether the government decides to tax 100 percent of your Social Security, but wouldn't you like to be one of those people who pays only 5, 10, or 15 percent for the rest of your life? I know what you're saying. You're asking, how do we go about doing that? Here's the key: <u>manage your taxes like you manage your assets</u>.

Remember: It's not how much you earn; it's how much you keep.

Whenever you think about that pile of retirement money you have, whether it's $500,000 or $1 million, you must understand that it is not all yours. In fact, the technical definition of an IRA is not an individual retirement **account**, as we tend to think, but rather an individual retirement **arrangement**. That's what it says in the tax code. You can find it described in Publication 590A from the Internal Revenue Service.

Why is that distinction so important? Think of it this way. An account is yours. If you have an account, you own it. But an arrangement is a contractual agreement between two or more parties. Who are the two parties in an IRA arrangement? They are you and the government. Also, the primary beneficiary on your IRA is not your spouse, it's the government, because you cannot disinherit the government from being a beneficiary on your retirement money. Or can you?

With proper planning, you can do a Roth IRA and disinherit the government. But that involves proactive planning. That's the one thing I want you to take away from this book: If you read this book or any other book on retirement planning and income planning, and you do not act upon it, it is time wasted.

The smartest people in the world all have coaches. I'm in New England, where there's a quarterback named TB that I'm pretty sure has several coaches.

We're all constantly learning and trying to improve ourselves. But what makes these people successful is that they take information and knowledge and put it to use. What's going to make you successful with your retirement is to take this knowledge and put it to use.

You need to manage your taxes like you manage your money and your wealth. Understand that taxes are going to be part of your retirement, and the best way to handle them is to deal with them now. Be proactive about it. Look at the opportunities you may have to reposition some of your assets and pay a little bit in taxes now, so that you don't have to pay as much, or anything, in the future.

PART II

Avoiding the Traps

Chapter 6

The Biggest Risks

RETIREMENT PLANNING IS a process, and in that process, there are some common risks to consider, myths to overcome, and mistakes to avoid.

The Five Risks of Retirement Planning

1. Market risk

That's the one most people think of first, and it's often the only one they think of in terms of retirement. Should I consider moving some money to safety as I approach retirement? What effect would a market correction like 2008 have on my portfolio? Consider what a 40-50 percent loss in your portfolio would do to your retirement income scenario, especially if you are near or recently retired. Will you have enough money to live on, and how long will it last? That is why it is so critical to understand that it may not be necessary to take big risks to get good returns. More on this later in this chapter.

2. Inflation risk

Some people are extremely risk adverse, and want all their money in guaranteed accounts, say like the bank, for example. You could argue that putting all your money in the bank keeps it safe in terms of your principal, but you are subjecting yourself to inflation risk. You are losing money to inflation every year. So that needs to be addressed. Now consider that Social Security has not kept pace with "real inflation" like the cost of groceries and fuel, and you begin to get the idea. So the real question is, how can we keep pace with inflation, without risking our principal? There is a potential solution to that question, and I will address it shortly.

3. Longevity risk

Longevity risk is exactly that. It is the risk of outliving your money. In fact, the number one concern among retirees is outliving their income. We need to make sure that our plan addresses that issue and makes sure that your check is going to be there for as long as you and your spouse need it. And the biggest threat today is that most folks' retirement assets are NOT guaranteed to last forever. We must include as part of our plan a guaranteed income stream along with Social Security to form the foundation of our income.

4. Health risk

That's the risk of getting sick, and needing home healthcare, long-term care, or assisted living care. As we mentioned earlier this is a very real but often ignored threat to our financial future. We need to at least discuss this, and have a contingency plan. And remember, your health insurance will not cover it.

5. Sequence of return risk

This is the risk of retiring at the "wrong" time. The best way to explain it is with the illustrations on the next pages

And as you can see, Bill and Sue each had $500,000, and they were each going to take six percent out of their pile. Bill happened to retire in 1990, and what you see below is the actual S&P 500 return from 1990 to 1999. Each year, Bill took $30,000 out of his portfolio, so after 10 years, he had taken out $300,000, but during that time his portfolio grew to over $1.2 million.

How? The truth is Bill just got lucky. He just happened to have his money in the market at the right time.

Sue had the same situation, starting with $500,000 in an IRA. She was born 10 years after Bill, so she retired in 2000, 10 years after Bill.

Unfortunately for Sue, the S&P was not so kind in those 10 years after she retired. At the end of those 10 years, after she had taken out her $300,000, she only had a little over $156,000 left. That's a scary situation. She's 10 years older and only has $156,000, but she needs $30,000 a year, and by the way, we didn't even account for inflation on that money.

None of this is Sue's fault; she just happened to retire at the wrong time. This sequence of return risk is a big risk that people often overlook. Proper planning eliminates the risk of running out of money and I will show you how later in this book.

SEQUENCE OF RETURNS:

Bill's Retirement

- Bill retires in 1990
- $500,000 in his IRA at retirement
- Withdrawing $30,000 annually for income

Year	Return	Withdrawal	Balance
1990	-4.34%	$ 30,000	$ 449,602
1991	20.32%	$ 30,000	$ 504,865
1992	4.17%	$ 30,000	$ 494,667
1993	13.72%	$ 30,000	$ 528,419
1994	2.14%	$ 30,000	$ 509,085
1995	33.45%	$ 30,000	$ 639,340
1996	26.01%	$ 30,000	$ 767,829
1997	22.64%	$ 30,000	$ 904,873
1998	16.10%	$ 30,000	$ 1,015,728
1999	25.22%	$ 30,000	$ 1,234,328

This is a hypothetical example that is demonstrating a mathematical principle. It does not illustrate any investment products and does not show past or future performance of any specific investment.

A TALE OF TWO (VERY DIFFERENT) RETIREMENTS

Sue's Retirement

- Sue retires in 2000
- $500,000 in her IRA at retirement
- Withdrawing $30,000 annually for income

Year	Return	Withdrawal	Balance
2000	-6.18%	$ 30,000	$ 440,954
2001	-7.10%	$ 30,000	$ 381,776
2002	-16.76%	$ 30,000	$ 292,819
2003	25.32%	$ 30,000	$ 329,364
2004	3.15%	$ 30,000	$ 308,794
2005	-0.61%	$ 30,000	$ 277,094
2006	16.29%	$ 30,000	$ 287,345
2007	6.43%	$ 30,000	$ 273,892
2008	-33.84%	$ 30,000	$ 161,359
2009	18.82%	$ 30,000	$ 156,081

This is a hypothetical example that is demonstrating a mathematical principle. It does not illustrate any investment products and does not show past or future performance of any specific investment.

Chapter 7

Myths and Mistakes

Now that you know what risks to consider, let's talk a bit about some of the other pitfalls that can trip up your retirement planning process. There are some very common myths about retirement planning, and unfortunately, they seem to be widely believed. I make it part of my mission with my clients to debunk these common beliefs, so let's take a moment to talk about them here.

Four Retirement Myths

Myth #1: The average return is my actual return.

This is the biggest myth I've seen, and it couldn't be further from the truth. In fact, I call it "the big lie." Why? Because no one has ever earned an average return, but it is allowed to be published. What is an average return? Let's look at an example. If you're up 20 percent and then you're down 20 percent, simple math says that your average return is zero. Right? Let's take it another step. If you're up 30 percent, and you're down 30 percent, again your average return is zero. That might be what the math says, but your actual return, or what we refer to as the geometric return, is a lot less. In fact, it's negative 9 percent on the 30 up, 30 down scenario.

I can hear you saying, "Wait a minute, Steve, up 30 and down 30 is zero." Yes, that's true in a simple math equation, but unfortunately, that simple math doesn't apply to your investments. And it explains why so many folks, when they lose money in the market, find it difficult to recover, particularly if they're drawing income. This is how it works in real life. Suppose you start with $100,000. If you are down 30 percent, you've lost $30,000, which means you now have $70,000 left. Let's say the next year is a good year and you earn 30 percent. So, 30 percent of $70,000 is $21,000, which added to your $70,000 brings you to only $91,000. You are down 9 percent from where you originally started. Yes, the average return is zero, but your actual return is negative 9 percent. And in case you're wondering, it works the same way if you are up year one and then down year two. Go ahead and try it. That's why we call this the big lie.

There's a website, www.MoneyChimp.com/features/market_cagr. htm, that offers a great tool for calculating the compound annual geometric return over a range of dates. For example, I went to Money Chimp and I plugged in January 1, 2000 to December 31, 2016. The average return on the S&P 500, including dividends, for 16 years, was 6.14 percent. However, the actual return that the investor got was only 4.47 percent—over a 16-year period.

It's eye-opening; I encourage you to try it. Throw in whatever years you want, and it will show you the average return and your actual return. Unfortunately, many financial planners will quote average returns, and when they do they're just not telling you the whole story.

Myth #2: You must take big risks in order to get a good return.

This one makes me chuckle. I've been in this business for over 30 years, I know the math, and I know that you don't have to take big risks to make good returns. I have customers who, since 2000, have been credited over 6 percent on their money without any direct downside market risk at all.[3] And since that time, not one of my clients has ever, ever lost a penny with me in any of those accounts that I have used. Not one client. I take a lot of pride in that. I take this job extremely seriously because folks are trusting me with their life savings. And if you're going to turn over your life savings to someone, you need to do your homework, and you need to know what you are getting back in return. What are the guarantees?

The bottom line is that you can take no market risk on your money and still have good returns. How? By using leverage. We'll talk about this in more detail elsewhere in this book, but basically, you use a vehicle that will allow you to participate in the upside of a growth index, but without participating in the negatives of it. While it's generally true that over the long haul the stock market has outpaced inflation, it carries no guarantees. And since we're retiring, or perhaps have already retired, we certainly don't want to have all our eggs in that one basket. At the same time, we certainly don't want to put our money under the mattress and lose to inflation and all those other risks that we talked about.

So, what is the answer? The answer is to use features from both. The answer is to utilize a market index, like the S&P 500, as a measuring stick in which you will be credited interest based on the movement of the selected market index. In a nutshell, if I were to say to you, "How about I offer you this? I'm going to credit you interest of 50 percent of any positive movement in the S&P 500 for a given year, but in return for that, I will eliminate all direct downside risk." Would you be interested in an account that would allow you to be credited interest for any gains in a market index, but never any of the losses? Most people that I speak to would say, "Of course." So, that myth is false. You can get good returns without taking any direct market risk.

Myth #3: You can do it yourself.

Many of us like to think, hey, I can do it myself. That's how I am. I'm in my 50s, and I'm that do-it-yourself guy. I built a beautiful stone walkway in my backyard. I built patios. I've done all kinds of improvements to my house. I'm proud of that, but when it comes to my money, I get this emotional attachment. We all do. We all operate on fear and greed. It's what motivates us when it comes to investing: fear, because I don't want to lose my money, and greed, because I want to make as much as I can, and don't want to miss out on an opportunity.

Those are two opposing forces colliding with one another. And when you put yourself in that pilot seat, trying to navigate your retirement plan yourself, you carry those emotions with you. We're all human. When the market goes up, we think it's because of us. We made a good call. And when the market crashes, what do we do? We panic. We say, "It crashed, and it could crash again. I don't want to lose anymore." And in that panic, people tend to pull their money out. You know the familiar adage: **"Buy low, sell high."** As of the writing of this book, the markets are at an all-time high, yet nobody—at least no one that I know of—is selling. But history repeats itself, and we don't want to be penny wise and pound foolish, particularly when it comes to our retirement plan.

When you're retired and you're taking an income, and your money gets hit for a 30 percent loss, the odds are that you will never recover your money. That's how you fall victim to that sequence of returns risk that we looked at on page [xxx]. So, let's play it smart and recognize that we all need help. We all need a coach.

I've been in this business 30 years, and when it comes to my own money, I use a coach. I have a money manager coach, because when it comes to my own plans, my Roth and my 401(k)s, I want to be emotionally unattached. I want to invest with logic, not emotion. That doesn't mean that you can't have some fun money. You know how I feel about buckets. I have one customer who has his e-trade account, and he calls that his fun bucket. That's his make-or-break account. He has fun; he does trades, but that account has no impact on his income check for him and his wife. None. Zero impact. It's a hobby for him and he enjoys it.

But retirement planning is not a hobby. Retirement planning—and having income for life—is serious. Trying to do it yourself can lead to a lot of emotional stress. You need to establish your foundation, and to do that, you want to work with an independent professional who is unemotionally attached from the situation. You want someone who can give you unbiased advice that is in your best interests. That's what we seek to do at my firm. I'll sit down with you, look at you in the eye, and say, "This is what you need to do. Here's why; here's how it works."

Even Tom Brady has a coach. In fact, he has several coaches. It's the same with us. We all need help; we all need coaches. It eliminates the emotion, creates a more successful environment, and allows us to participate in the process.

Myth #4: It's too good to be true.

I hear this a lot, especially at workshops when I talk about some of the specialized products that we're going to get into. People say, "Steve, it's too good to be true. It sounds too good to be true; there's no way it could be that way." The other line that goes with this one is, "Steve, if it's so good, why isn't everybody doing it?" I love that line. My answer is always that not everybody knows about it, or not everybody takes advantage of it.

That's why I provide this book, my seminars, and my radio show. I want all my readers, listeners, and people who come in to see me to understand that there are different methodologies, different ways to retire, and different products out there. The only way you're going to find out about them is to get educated and look at the numbers.

The fact is: **It's not too good to be true; it's too good to be free.** We all know that there is no free lunch; everything comes with its pros and its cons. I'm biased, like everyone else, and this is my bias: I want my customers to have a check that is guaranteed to last for their lifetime, and/or their spouses, so that they can enjoy and do the things they want to do during their retirement years.

My other bias is that I don't want my clients to ever, ever lose a nickel they have invested with me to downside market risk. But nothing is free, so we present all the facts so that my clients understand how these products work. Ultimately, I believe guaranteed income should be more important than the possibility of potential gains.

Knowledge is power, but knowledge combined with action is even more powerful. Many of the folks I've talked to over the years have taken advantage of what I had to say. Others have not. Even though I've armed them with the knowledge, they didn't act on it. My advice is to verify the facts, and make a decision that helps you and your family gain greater financial confidence.

Six Common Mistakes to Avoid

Mistake #1: Using the wrong tool

One of the most common mistakes I see is lumping your accumulation products and your future income products together, making the mistake of thinking you can use the same tool to accomplish a completely different objective.

What do I mean by that? While you're still working, and you still have time on your side, whether it's five years or 10 years, you're in growth mode—what we call accumulation mode. You're in a deferred mode because your working income—your salary or earnings—is your source of income. In that mode, most people want to strive for growth of their portfolio.

Like a farmer, you're still planting the seeds. But when it comes time to harvest—once you get to that point and you retire—you can't harvest the seeds using the same methodology that you used to plant them. Or maybe you're in construction and you're framing a house. To do that you're using a framing hammer, a heavier hammer, and bigger nails to set the foundation. But when you get to the finish work, you're going to need a completely different set of tools. You may still be using a hammer, but it's going to be smaller. The nails are going to be different and finer. It's the same thing with your retirement plan. Your accumulation is now going to become your income, so instead of requiring your portfolio to keep growing, you're now demanding that your portfolio produce an income check to replace your salary.

And you can't address that need with an accumulation vehicle only, or you're going to run the risk of running out of money. It's that simple. If you have the wrong tools to try to do the job, you're going to have risk in your portfolio. That's going to put stress on the portfolio, and that may lead towards stress in your life. We want to reduce that stress, not increase it. I will share some great income tools later in this book that I have used to successfully produce lifetime income, with no direct downside market risk.

Mistake #2: Systematic withdrawals

The second common mistake I see ties in with the first one. It's the use of systematic withdrawals, taking a withdrawal from a bucket which carries with it financial uncertainty, versus using a vehicle that guarantees income, with a contractual obligation. When you use a systematic withdrawal, you are triggering an income for yourself that may or may not happen. When you do that, there is nothing in writing to guarantee that the income will be there.

Most of these products have a disclaimer that says past performance is no guarantee of future results. I don't know about you, but when I retire, the last thing I want to see is a disclaimer that says, you can take your income, but we don't know if it's going to be there in the next five, 10, or 15 years. I get a little nervous about that. I'd rather have something in writing.

Compare that situation to a guarantee or a contract. A contractual obligation is ironclad. So, imagine, when you retire, instead of getting a maybe, you get a guarantee in writing that income will be there not only for you, but for your spouse, if you so choose. It is a promise in writing, and it is backed by billion-dollar companies. A solid foundation. When you build a house, you want your foundation to be as solid as possible. You want it to be made of concrete. If the foundation is weak, your house is weak—it's that simple. It's the same with your retirement plan. Guaranteed Income opposed to potential IFcome.

Mistake #3: When to take Social Security

The third common mistake I see is taking Social Security either too early or too late.

If taken at the wrong time, Social Security can be a $100,000 to $150,000 mistake. And unlike other choices that you make in retirement, once you do it, it can't be undone. You can have your money in the wrong plan, get a second opinion, and fix it, but once you make that Social Security election, that's it. And if you made that choice already, then you need to make sure the rest of the plan addresses it. We covered this subject a lot in the Pension and Social

Security section, but this is one mistake we want to be sure we avoid, and getting all the numbers is crucial.

Mistake #4: Underestimating taxes

The fourth mistake I see is not taking tax planning into account when it comes to your income. I keep saying this, but I can't stress it enough: **It's not what you earn, it's what you keep.**

You can have a vast plan, with multiple pieces here and there, but those monies can cause your income to be taxed at a higher rate because of how it is distributed. Maybe, for example, you would do better to defer Social Security and spend down some of your taxable monies when you first retire, so that in the future you can take a higher guaranteed check and less of a total taxable check.

It's very common for folks, when they retire, to take their Social Security and pension election if they have one, at the same time. Then roll over their 401(k) or their 403(b) into an IRA and just kind of go from there. That's the typical plan that I see. When people come in, they hand me statements. They're generally assets under management, usually at some big firm. It usually has fees attached to it, and in most cases, it comes with no guarantees. Not understanding how each of these pieces effect your taxes could be a major mistake, but one that may be fixed, even if you are already retired. It's never too late to plan.

Mistake #5: Failing to diversify

This is the fifth mistake I see: keeping all your eggs in one basket. You might say, "Steve, they're not really in all one basket because I have a managed portfolio of stocks and bonds," but you're still in that one same basket. In other words, that basket is all subject to risk. Or, that basket might be a 100 percent taxable basket like an IRAs or a 401(k). You need to diversify properly by having your assets in different categories so that you're in control of your retirement and not the government. Remember the four types of money: FREE, TAX-FREE, TAX-DEFERRED, and TAXABLE.

With a 401(k) or an IRA, your partner is the government. Because of that, you lose tax control, because at 70 and a half, and the government requires you to take minimum distributions.

Therefore, you want to diversify your assets not only for tax purposes, but for control. And we want to define and label those buckets to address income, emergencies, travel and inflation.

Mistake #6: Working with the wrong planner

The sixth common retirement planning mistake that I see is working with the wrong planner. Yes, you read that right—working with the wrong financial professional. You need the right specialist.

When people retire, they tend to maintain the same person who may have helped them in previous years, a 401(k) administrator or a manager of the IRA they had. They assume that person is going to be qualified to help them in this new phase of their lives, but retirement income planning is a completely different discipline from accumulation planning.

It's like anything else. As we get older things change. When we're kids, we go to a pediatrician. When we get older, we go to a different doctor, maybe a primary care physician, maybe a specialist. It no longer makes sense for us to go to a doctor who specializes in treating kids. Our health needs a different kind of care.

Think of your money the same way. When we're younger, we treat it very differently than when we're older. Our needs change, and so we need to see a different specialist. Most folks make the mistake of using the same person they used during their accumulation years, and that person may not be the best qualified to help them once they move into the decumulation stage. As a retirement income certified professional, that is the exact area that I specialize in. In fact, I very rarely work with anybody under 50 years old. It's a different discipline, with different tools. There are many ways of taking income and making sure it lasts, so you want to be working with a specialist.

I make it a very large part of my practice to educate folks and make them aware that retirement planning is completely different than saving money. It's not about saving. It's about preserving the asset and the income that it can and will provide. It's about how long that income is guaranteed to be provided, what happens in the event of a death, how a spouse will be protected, and how an estate will be administered. It's about creating a well-thought-out plan that takes into consideration not only the income that you're going to need but also the goals and the dreams that you have for your retirement.

I can't stress enough how much people enjoy coming into my office, sitting in my conference room, with my white board there on the wall and having me draw out for them their future, their income, their buckets if you will. They love it. With the couples, it's so fun to see their expressions especially when some of them say to me, "Well, Steve, you know that bucket looks great, but boy, I want my fun bucket to be bigger. How can we make that happen?" Those are the conversations you want to have when you retire. Where is my fun bucket, how is that going to be positioned, how much access am I going to have to it, what are the tax consequences? Hey, Steve, when I'm 65 I'm going to need this much income, when I'm 70 I'm going to need an inflation hedge, and where's this income going to come from? How long is that going to last? How's it going to work when I'm 75?

I ladder it for them. Ladder one might be for the next five years, ladder two might be from year six all the way to the future and so on. By doing that, creating that retirement blueprint, they're going to see their hopes, their dreams, and their goals actually come alive. That's the type of planner you want to work with: somebody who specializes, somebody who has knowledge in that field. You want somebody who is independent and can represent the companies that are available in that particular space so that the consumer is getting options from all these different companies, because companies out there have niches too. For example, a lot of mutual fund companies are now selling annuities. It doesn't mean they're good at it. It just means that they're offering those as a piece of what they're doing. Anytime I see that happen, I consider it a red flag.

Banks are selling annuities too. Their products may be okay, but they don't specialize in income planning. Banks specialize in safety and liquidity—CDs, money markets, checking and saving. I recently had a client come in who said, "I just visited the bank and they suggested I put my CDs into this annuity." When I looked at the proposal, it was paying two, two and a half percent which was more than the CD, but it didn't address the income planning need, and it disinherited the spouse!

This is why you should consider an independent professional who specializes in income planning.

So those are the common mistakes I've seen, and don't worry for those of you who are just about to retire, we can talk about it. For those of you who are already retired, it's never too late. Second opinions are important. Whether you're 65, 70, or 75, there's still time to make changes to your portfolio to provide income and ensure a legacy plan if need be.

Let's keep that in mind as we enter the next step, putting all the pieces together to create the best possible plan for you and your family, putting you on a path towards greater financial peace of mind now and throughout your retirement years.

PART III

Putting Yourself on the Green

Chapter 8

Your Own Buckets of Wealth

LET'S RECAP. We've set the table by gathering all the individual pieces. We have our Social Security, our pensions, our retirement monies, which are our 401(k)s, 403(b)s, IRAs, etc. We have our health insurance information. We have all our paperwork, and now we have a basic understanding of why taxes play a role. The next step is to establish your buckets of wealth and fund them.

Establishing Your Buckets of Wealth

The first thing you're going to need is income. That's why we're doing this exercise—to come up with income for the rest of your life to replace the income you have been getting from your job during your working years, or to guarantee more income if you are already retired. We need an **income bucket**. It's the most important bucket, and it needs to be stable. It needs to be a pillar. It needs to be guaranteed.

Next, we need to establish what I refer to as an **inflation hedge bucket**. As the name implies, we aren't necessarily going to take money from that bucket right now, but it is there to keep pace with inflation. As the years go by we drip a little out of that bucket to keep your checks in line with inflation.

Next, we have the **fun/travel bucket**. It's the reason why you've worked hard all your life. What's the point of working so hard and saving your money if you're not going to have fun with it? If you're not going to travel? If you're not going to do the things that you've always wanted to do over the last 20 or 30 years? When you meet with me, we sit and chat about those things. We're going to talk about making sure that you have that fun money and that travel money because that's really what it's all about.

Having said that, you also need to have your **emergency bucket**. Things don't always go as we plan, so you need to have money set aside somewhere safe and somewhere liquid just in case, for example, your roof needs repair, or you need a new car. Maybe you have an added assessment on a property, or you get hit with a storm. There's always going to be something to anticipate or account for.

The reason I emphasize these different buckets is that you don't want to have everything in one single bucket and then pull from it for different reasons. If you do that you're not going to be able to take advantage of proper tax and income planning.

Here's an example. Suppose you put all your money in one bucket because you thought it was the better return, and then you had an emergency where you needed $10,000, or $20,000, or $50,000? And at that same time, the market crashed 30 percent! Well, that's a bad time to pull from that bucket. If something goes wrong, you want to draw from your worst account first. That's going to be your emergency bucket, your savings bucket. The price you pay for having safety and liquidity is a lower rate of return, but it enables you to invest in the other buckets knowing that if there's an emergency, you don't have to tap those at the wrong time. You can allow those other buckets to do their job.

Lastly, you may want to establish a **legacy bucket**. How can I leave what's left to my family in the most tax-efficient way possible? That's the question, and there are fantastic vehicles that allow you to do so not only TAX-FREE, but for pennies on the dollar. Leveraging your money allows you to enjoy more now and pass more later tax efficiently.

Filling the Buckets

Once you have your buckets determined, you can start putting all the pieces together.

Once we have an idea of what your income needs are, we look at your pension options, if you have one. If you are already retired, we use those numbers, along with any survivor benefits. If you are still working, we need to look at your options. Do you take the Option A and buy your own life insurance, or is the company's plan a better way to provide a survivor option?

After we tackle that, we address Social Security. If you are already retired, we use your existing numbers. If not, then do you take Social Security early, take it at full retirement age, or defer it till age 70? The answer to that question will depend on your other assets, income, and your health. If you're married, we also must take into consideration those benefits and whose check is the larger one, because when one spouse dies, the smaller Social Security check is forfeited. Social Security is a permanent decision once you take the check, so we want to get it right. It's all about sitting down, running the numbers, and then making an informed, intelligent decision.

Next, we move on to the 401(k)s, the 403(b)s, and the IRAs. Do you leave your employer-sponsored plan where it is, or do you take that plan and roll it over to your own personally-controlled IRA? It's going to depend on many factors; fees, the choice of funds that your employer offers, and convenience. If you've been with two or three employers, you might have two or three different 401(k)s or 403(b)s, and that could be confusing to keep track of. With an IRA, however, you would be able to combine those and have one account. Again, you take the pieces, ask the questions, run down the different scenarios, and act accordingly.

In the end the goal is to have a well-thought-out plan that addresses income, taxes, inflation, and legacy planning with the flexibility to adapt to changing circumstances. The foundation is **lifetime income**, so my goal is to establish that first, and build everything else around it. And to do so I firmly believe everyone needs to have a rock-solid foundation that includes the "secret sauce" in the next chapter.

Chapter 9

The Essential Retirement Toolkit

I BELIEVE THAT everyone should have at least one of these tools in their retirement plan. I consider them my "secret sauce"—essential tools to a successful retirement income plan.

Index annuities[4]

Earlier in the book, I talked about establishing buckets: an income bucket, an inflation hedge bucket, an emergency bucket, and a fun bucket. Your income bucket must have guarantees, and index annuities are a great way of accomplishing that. It's a bit like having your cake and eating it too.

Why do I say that? An index annuity allows individuals to earn interest credits based on the movement of a market index while having no direct downside market risk. We take calculated risks in our lives, particularly when we're younger, so that our money will hopefully outpace inflation, while allowing us to take advantage of compound interest.

When we're near retirement or in retirement, the risk factor becomes more important. It looms larger in the background. The last thing we want to do is to retire at the wrong time, and get caught in a bad sequence of return. You could retire and then have the market collapse that same year. That could be devastating to your entire income plan and could even force you back to work. We don't want to do that.

We want to take advantage of the opportunity for growth, but we also want to eliminate that direct downside risk. At the same time, we don't want to take our money and leave it under a mattress or in the bank and run the risk of losing to inflation.

Picture yourself in a huge department store. You're on the first floor and you step on the escalator to go to a higher floor. Think of the index annuity as a way of taking an escalator towards retirement instead of a roller coaster. An escalator will go up. At some point, it may pause. The same goes for the stock market. At some point, your market takes a tumble. And when that market goes down, this escalator pauses at that particular floor, and we're just going to wait patiently right there. Rather than having to go all the way back down to the first floor to try to get to the third floor, we're going to wait on the second floor. And when the market recovers, we're going to proceed from the second floor to the third.

An old adage says we take two steps forward and one step back. We want to eliminate that one step back. We want to take the escalator instead of the roller coaster. Let's face it, we all love the idea of market opportunities, but we hate the thought of not being able to protect our principal. So why not protect that principal while being credited interest in reference to the movement of a market index? And that's the idea.

As I mentioned, this is an income bucket. Not only can this product keep pace when the market's up and protect you when the market's down, it can also provide an income for the rest of your lifetime, guaranteed in writing. That's something you really can't get from a true investment. It's really a novel concept, which can provide greater peace of mind for both spouses.

Will Rogers once said, "I am more concerned with the return of my money, than the return on my money." That's never truer than when you approach retirement. We know right now, as of the writing of this book, the market is good. As a matter of fact, it's at an all-time high. But it wasn't raining when Noah built the ark. The time to plan, and the time to take action, is before an event happens.

The purpose of this product is to get you out of the way of the rainstorm before it occurs. You're probably thinking, "Steve, that sounds way too good to be true." Remember what I said about the myths of retirement planning? It's not too good to be true. I started doing these back in 1999, and I got so excited about what these products could do for my clients that I literally stopped offering products in the markets, like mutual funds and such. I stopped doing those in 2004 because this tool was so powerful in filling my income bucket. I could not find an alternative that would give me a better solution.

Remember our original question from the beginning of this book. Why do we work so hard and save all this money? Because we want future income to replace our current working income.

And what's our greatest fear in retirement? Outliving our income. Can you imagine you're 82, or 83, or 85, and you have all your money in the inflation hedge bucket, and you're drawing an income from that, and 2008 happens all over again? The economy crashes again and you lose half that money. What would you do? You certainly can't take the same amount of money from half the pile. You'll run out of money. Then what? You're 84, you're 85, and the only thing you have left is possibly Social Security. That's a scary scenario. Unfortunately, I've seen people go through it, and I have vowed that it's never going to happen to my clients.

So here's another question: What is the only product offered in the United States that guarantees an income check that you will never outlive? The answer is an annuity. So that being the case, the secret sauce is to use an annuity product that can give a check and then allow that product to calculate interest in reference to the movement of a market index that will give you greater growth than say a money market or a CD. Think about it. Think about having the opportunity to be credited interest based on the movement of the market and never directly participate in the downside of the market. So how is that for your later bucket? That's the bucket where you're still working and you're putting this money in, and then at four, five, six, seven, eight years, whatever the number, you can turn that bucket on and convert it to a check for life that will pay not only for you, but also for your spouse. On the second death, the proceeds, if anything is left, go to your beneficiary of choice, not to the company that issued the annuity.

Over the years I've done index annuities for hundreds and hundreds of clients. I can honestly assure you, as of this writing, that not one of them has lost a nickel from direct market risk, even though we have had two major downturns since 1999.

So number one in the toolbox is the income bucket and it's called an index annuity. It is an amazing product that can offer you that check you need for life, and it can offer you the opportunity for growth without any direct downside risk. It's one of my essentials when I build a plan, and I strive to build a rock-solid retirement plan.

If you would like to know more about index annuities, I have some great resources in my office that offer much more detail. Contact my office through www.fairwayfinancial.net and we can help carve out for you a very personalized approach to this great tool.

Tax-free leverage

This is the second piece of the retirement toolkit, after lifetime income. The tax-free bucket is extremely valuable for business owners in their 40s, 50s and even early 60s. It can also be valuable for other folks, even non-business owners, who are conservative and who have a lot of cash in the bank, in CDs, or in brokerage accounts that they're getting taxed on every year.

You may have guessed that there's another name for this tax-free bucket. It's called life insurance. Now again, before you decide I'm crazy and close this book, take a moment to read on. What does life insurance have to do with retirement planning? Everything—the whole idea of life insurance is exactly that. It insures your life from living too long or from dying too soon. It uses the very tools that corporate America uses. Banks, insurance companies, and very astute, wealthy individuals use this, taking advantage of the concepts of arbitrage and leverage.

Arbitrage is essentially a way of using other people's money to make money for yourself. If you think about it, that's what banks do, right? You put your money in your bank, they give you a set interest rate, and then they in turn lend the money out to someone else at a higher interest rate to buy a home, or a car, or some other purchase. The bank uses your money to make money for the bank. That's called arbitrage. Leverage is similar. It's the ability to take a dollar and make it do two or three different tasks. It's about making your money work not only harder, but smarter, and today that is more important than ever.

Let me explain why life insurance is such a great tool for this, whether you're already in retirement, close to retirement, or nearing retirement. Remember what we said about putting together the pieces of your retirement, such as Social Security and a pension, if you have one. We learned that, depending on what pension option you take, you're going to have a gap. If you take a pension option with no survivor benefit and you die, you're leaving nothing behind. Even if you take a 50 percent survivor benefit, you're going to have a gap. We also learned that with Social Security, the surviving spouse of a married couple will lose a check. It'll be the smaller of the two, fortunately, but nonetheless it will be a lost check. How do we replace that check, and how can we do that for pennies on the dollar? See, this is the real key. This leverage bucket, or life insurance bucket, is an amazing tool to take nickels and turn them into hundreds, tax-free, for the survivor. So that's one reason why this is an amazing planning tool.

The other reason this is such an amazing tool is that you can use life insurance to create an instant, tax-free estate. Remember that legacy bucket we talked about earlier? This is a way to fill that bucket, even for someone who has moderate means, maybe half a million or a million in total assets. This is an opportunity to leverage those assets by taking a piece and creating an instant, tax-free estate for pennies on the dollar.

When you look at these first two tools, don't let the names get in the way. Let go of what you've heard or what you think you know, and really look at the benefits. In my experience, people love the benefits of index annuities and they love the benefits of life insurance. They just dislike the names. If you can throw the name out the window and just look at the benefits, then your eyes open up to the possibilities.

Here's an example. I see lots of clients, let me tell you about one in particular. I'll call her Rose. As I'm writing this book, she just left my office. Rose is very fortunate. She has a large pension, $3,200/month. She also has her Social Security, which is $2,800/month. So here's Rose, in her mid-70s, with $6,000/month of guaranteed income with no debt.

Rose also has another half million dollars. Now she happened to have it in a variable annuity, which I'm not a huge fan of, but it does have a guaranteed income. The irony is that she doesn't need the income. She just got her RMD check of $25,000, and she literally walked into my office the other day with the check in her hand.

She said, "I don't know what to do with this." After I cracked up laughing, I said, "Cash it. Put it in your bank." But as we talked we came up with another plan. Rose said, "Steve, I'm very fortunate. I don't need the money, but I can't stand the fact that I've got to pay taxes on it."

I laughed again and said, "Well, how about I put it in my bank?" She had talked to me earlier about her five nephews and nieces who will be her heirs. I said, "Let's take this money and make sure that it passes to them as tax efficiently as possible."

Well, she had a pretty good never bucket. I said, "If we work with that money alone, I can leverage it. I can take about $20,000 of it after taxes and I can create an instant estate of over $200,000 tax-free." She was shocked. She said that no other advisor had ever suggested told her about that. I said, "Well, that's the difference between a retirement specialist and someone who calls themselves an advisor."

So this is another unbelievable use for life insurance, **IRA rescue**. We can rescue your IRA from taxes so that you can spend every nickel of it during your lifetime and replace it totally tax-free for either your spouse or any other beneficiary that you choose, whether it be a church or your children or your grandchildren.

What about tax-free income for life? As I explained earlier, when it comes to 401(k)s and IRAs the government is your partner. They want their share. However, using life insurance for lifetime income is the last great tax shelter available in America. Think of it as a Roth IRA with unlimited potential. Business owners, by the way, take note: you can do this just for yourself, or you can do it for your key employees.

For us regular working folks, this is an unbelievable opportunity to take money you have set aside and put it into a tax-free account where it will grow tax-deferred and very similar to an index annuity where your interest credit is based upon the growth of an index. Most of these products use the S&P 500 and interest is calculated in reference to its movement. I have very detailed histories on these products.

Max-funded life

If you couple that with tax-free it's even more phenomenal. This is a very special strategy, called **max-funded insurance.** Not many people have heard of this, but I think it's an extremely valuable tool if you are able to do it. That may depend on time; usually these types of products take a little more time to grow. But I believe in this so much that I'm doing it as part of my own retirement plan.

This is another vehicle that, like an indexed annuity, credits interest in reference to the movement of a market index and never directly participates in the downside market movement. Max-funded life insurance is a particular shelter in which your money grows tax-deferred, but you can access it tax-free.[5] It's almost like a super-charged Roth IRA, but it has an insurance benefit, a life insurance death benefit. You can have a self-completing plan that would defer your money safely and have the opportunity to grow and credit interest based on the growth of a market index. Let's say you started this plan in your late 50s and early 60s and you pass away prior to reaching your retirement. This plan would pay off a life insurance policy tax-free to your spouse or beneficiary to self-complete the plan. In other words, we use leverage. Can you imagine putting in $100,000 and having this thing be worth $250,000 instantly tax-free to complete your plan in the event of your death?

This can be a good tool for income planning. Remember it's not just what you earn, but what you keep, so tax-free is really good. Think about our four categories: free, tax-free, tax-deferred, and taxable. This falls into the tax-free category. So can you imagine supplementing your Social Security and a pension, if you're lucky enough to have one, with another source of tax-free income for life? It's an amazing tool. A lot of people do not know about this, and unfortunately a lot of people in my industry are not trained enough in this product to explain it properly to be able to offer it correctly. I have taken specialized training for this, and I have applied it not only in my own situation, but in many of my clients' situations as well. There is no one product that fits all, obviously, but this has been a great supplement.

Most of these plans require a minimum of five or six years to grow, but after that they will provide a nice lifetime income check. I know you're thinking, how can life insurance pay me an income? That's the million-dollar question. Here's the answer: Life insurance is not just for your beneficiaries; it's for you too.

Most people don't understand that you can become your own beneficiary of your own life insurance policy. How? You do it by max funding the life insurance. And what exactly does that mean? Let me explain it with an analogy. I'm going to paint the picture as if you were an investor in real estate.

Suppose you buy a five-unit condo complex, planning to rent it out so that you can get income for life. Of course, you're probably going to have a mortgage and that's likely to be expensive, so let's say you buy the building and you rent the first floor and the second floor. That's pretty much going to cover your basic expenses and your costs.

Let's compare that situation to life insurance. Most people spend the least amount they can on the most amount of life insurance. What they get for that is called term insurance. As the name implies, term insurance runs out at a certain date, at the end of its term. Insurance companies love term insurance because they rarely have to pay the policy out. That's why it's the least expensive. It's like just funding the first floor of your condo building.

If you fund the second floor, you're going to cover the cost of the life insurance for longer than a period of five or 10 or 15 years. You might even cover it for as long as you live. But that's not really going to provide you with an income, because you're barely covering the expenses of the policy. That's the next stage of a typical policy, and that's called universal life, or guaranteed term life. It will last about as long as you do, and you just pay a little higher premium. But it doesn't really do much for you. But when you start to overfund the policy, now you're funding the third floor and the fourth floor and the fifth floor. Think about that as a real estate investor.

That third floor puts you 100 percent even—all the money you're putting in is pretty much going to come back to you. Now you're getting a return on your premium. Not a great investment, but you're basically breaking even. It's the fourth and fifth floor where the money is. That's the income. In that real estate investment with five units, ultimately once you fund the five floors, that's money in the bank. When you max fund a life insurance policy, you fund it to the maximum allowable amount, so you're now you're doing what we call overfunding. That means you're putting more money towards the investment part and less money towards the life insurance part. That's where the money can really grow, and defer, and compound.

Then down the road, whether it's six years, seven years, or ten years from now, you can turn on the money because you've over-funded it. In other words, you've put so much more into it. Instead of paying a little bit of premium for a lot of life insurance, you want to pay a lot of premium for a little bit of life insurance. As we like to say in our business, the life insurance part comes along for the ride. That keeps the cost down and keeps the investment up, so in the end, instead of dying to get a benefit, you can now use all the cash value that has grown in that policy.

And here's the wonderful part about arbitrage. Now we're going to use that money to create a loan to ourselves. We're literally going to pay ourselves our own money, and because it's a loan, it's tax-free income. This is a brilliant, tried-and-true strategy that has been around for over 100 years.

As a matter of fact, Walt Disney is a great example of someone who actually used cash value on his life insurance policies when he first started his theme parks. That actually carried him through. The great minds out there know about these products. They understand them. That's why the wealthiest people in the world own the most life insurance—because they understand leverage and arbitrage. And now you can do it too, and make it part of your plan.

I know these concepts may be new to you, but I hope that's why you're reading this book—to learn how to develop your ultimate retirement plan. As you can see, life insurance is a very effective tool for retirement planning. It can be used in many situations: to replace lost checks, to create an instant tax-free estate, to rescue your IRA from taxes to your beneficiaries, and ultimately to provide you with tax-free income for life. And by the way, even when you have taken that income and you pass away, there is still a tax-free death benefit that is payable to your spouse or to your children.

Of course, we're all about knowledge here at Fairway Financial, and I'd be happy to custom tailor a plan based on your personal situation. I can educate you about the process and show you directly how these benefits can work for you.

Linked-benefit or Hybrid bucket

This is our third essential tool. We spoke of this earlier in our long-term care insurance section, but it bears repeating since it has gained so much popularity in the last 5–10 years as the ultimate sleep-at-night asset protection vehicle.

After 30 years in this business, I have found that, most often, the reason people have large amounts of money saved somewhere is in case they get sick and need long-term care. It's as simple as that.

We touched on that earlier in this book. Long-term care coverage is a real threat.

If you are sick longer than 100 days, your medical plan is not going to pay. You're going to need some form of long-term care. People don't want to think about that. I've heard it a million times: "I'm never going to get sick. I'm never going to a nursing home. I'm never going to need this money."

We need to look at the reality. What's really going to happen in your life? I see three possibilities.

The first is that you could live a long and healthy life. You might even live to 90 or 95. The second is that you could die too soon. The third is we could become disabled and need long-term care.

So, is there a tool out there that can address all of these contingencies? Believe it or not, there actually is. It's called a linked-benefit life product, and addresses each of these three contingencies.

If you live a long life, it will act as your emergency savings account, giving you 100 percent access, with no penalties or fees.

Now consider the **Hybrid Option:** so if you ever decide you don't want this, you will get your money back. It's very simple. Why is the insurance company so generous? Because when you die, it they are going to guarantee to step up that check, say for example, to $120,000. That's 20 percent more than you would have if you left it in the bank. You would have to live about 20 years for the bank money to be worth $120,000. With this product, we're going to guarantee that $120,000 the day you give us $100,000. Talk about leverage—right away, your account is worth 20 percent more.

Lastly, what if you get sick, become disabled, and need long-term care? Unfortunately, it's a real possibility. Remember, statistics say that couples age 65 have a 40 percent chance of one spouse needing some form of long-term care, whether it be home healthcare, adult daycare, assisted living, or nursing home care.

Here is where this option gets really interesting. What happens to your $100,000? Well if you bought this product at age 62, a $100,000 deposit would have produced $3,600 a month tax-free for six years to be used towards your long-term care! That's a total of $259,200 over six years.

If we added an inflation rider, at age 80 this product would pay you almost $7000 a month for six years, which is $84,000 a year, all of it tax-free. That's a little over $500,000, for a one-time $100,000 deposit.

That, folks, is leverage. That is peace of mind, knowing that you can take your savings bucket, that money earning 1 percent, and have it protect your other assets. Otherwise, what good is all the other planning we have talked about if a nursing home wipes out your life savings?

And why is it becoming so popular the last few years?

Because traditional long-term care insurance is becoming harder to qualify for, it can be very expensive, and if you never use it, you never recover your premiums.

Suppose you buy a long-term care policy for maybe $6,000 a year. At age 65, the likelihood you'll need it right away isn't great. In ten years, that will be $60,000 out the door. In 15 years, that's $90,000 you'll never see again if you haven't yet used the policy.

Our hybrid bucket, on the other hand, has power. If you never use it, you eventually get your money back in the form of a death benefit, guaranteed.

Another problem with traditional long-term care is the incredible amount of premium increases. I can testify to that because, unfortunately, I have seen a lot of my clients experience it. The companies can raise the premiums, and some of the increases are outrageous.

I just got a notice from a major insurance company for one of my clients. This particular contract was issued in 2004. The insurance company filed for an increase of 31.49 percent. The state of Massachusetts capped them at a 20 percent increase. And this is not the first increase this client has had. So here's this woman, at close to 80 years old, getting her premium raised by 20 percent.

Think that's bad? Here's another one. This policy was issued in 2001. This client is now in his 80s. The insurance company called for an increase of 181.97 percent! The state capped it at 40 percent. So this man, in his 80s, got a 40 percent increase in his long-term care policy. Obviously, at his age, he's never going to be able to get that coverage again. What choice does the man have? He needs to take it. He needs to pay it. Otherwise, he loses the coverage.

Why do I put so much emphasis on these essential tools? Because retirement planning has changed. It is not just about the bells and the whistles, the stock of the week and the fund of the week, and my portfolio with all its managed assets. That's the last thing it's about.

Retirement planning is the process of putting together the pieces of the puzzle to create a guaranteed income for life, to replace the working income that you had. These essential tools, address the reality of what retirement planning is today. That is to protect what you have, to provide an income for life, and to pass on what's left as tax efficiently as possible. That has now become the ideal model of a solid retirement plan, and you need at least one of those tools in your retirement toolkit to help you create that plan.

Putting the toolkit to work: Bill and Helen's story

Bill and Helen were already retired when they came to me. They were in their early 70s, and they had two young grandkids, aged 9 and 6. Bob and Helen's goal was to create a college fund for their grandkids. They had very specific criteria. The fund had to be something that a) they had control over, b) would grow tax-deferred, and c) would be able to be pulled out to use for their grandkids' education without disrupting their kids' college FAFSA forms. They wanted to be able to save money and give their kids money for the grandkids, without it affecting the financial aid.

I said, "Okay, let me think about this." What we came up with was, I think, one of my best plan designs ever. We were able to fund a special insurance product that paid at the second death, not the first, but the second. Every other advisor they saw said, "Oh, just throw your money into mutual funds and then you can pull it out later." But that didn't meet their definition of safe, tax-deferred, and then available tax-free for their grandkids with control.

I told them I had the answer—a **self-completing plan**. I explained that they would give me a deposit every year and we would put it into this program. We would insure both of them for the cost of both educations, which we had determined to be somewhere around $640,000. Bill and Helen travel all the time, all over the world, so I said, "If you folks travel and something should happen to both of you, while you're traveling, this plan will be self-completing. It will provide the funds instantly in a trust for the benefit of your grandkids." Bill said, "Well, I like that." Then I told him, "It gets better. The money you put in will go into a tax-deferred account that can take advantage of the market gains and never any losses." He said, "I like that, too."

Then I gave him the third benefit. I said, "When you pull the money out, you can pull it out tax-free for the benefit of your grand-kids. And if your grandkids don't go to college, you can pull it out for whatever reason you want—for yourself, for your own children, maybe for the grandkids to help them buy their first house, if they decide not go to college. Let's say they want to go into plumbing or electrical or trades. You can help them there." They said it was exactly what they were looking for. We underwrote the product a few years back and they are thrilled. That's just one use of the max index life policy, max-funded.

So these are my two secret sauces that I believe all retirees should consider before they make any final decisions: indexed annuity and max-funded life insurance. They can really help you put the pieces together and enhance your blueprint.

Chapter 10

Your Retirement Blueprint

WHETHER YOU ARE still working, or already retired, you need a blueprint. When we get together, you'll find that I'm going to ask a lot of questions about your income, your goals, your travel plans, and more. I'll ask whether you're going to purchase a second home, whether you're going to stay where you are and just travel about, what you're going to need for emergency accounts, and so on. Then I'm going to put together a rough blueprint. So just like you have a blueprint when you build a home, we're going to have that same blueprint when we build your life's retirement income plan. It's going to be a rough draft first and we're going to build it together. I'm going to show you where you're at now, what cash flow you're going to need in the future, how we're going to account for inflation, and we're going to lay it all out for you on paper.

The Color of Money

People love to see that first blueprint. It just makes them feel that they're on the right track. You realize you're not as confused as you were before even though we're talking about many issues. You can tell yourself, "I'm here with Steve and he's really being my quarterback. He's helping me get through all this and answer these questions logically and unemotionally, so we can make some intelligent decisions."

And perhaps even more fun is when we assign colors to the assets. When my clients receive their blueprint, I color-code it so clients can see where their money is now and where it may be suited going forward.

RED represents risk, so any assets that are subject to risk are in shown in RED. Safe low return money like savings, checking and money market accounts are shown in BLUE, and our essential toolkit products, because they eliminate the direct downside risk, but also offer upside potential and lifetime income, are shown in GREEN.

This literally helps paint a good picture of where they are today and where it may benefit them to be in the future.

Cash flows are also color coded to show guaranteed income versus non-guaranteed income. This is to show the foundation of the plan and potential income from other sources, and customers find it extremely helpful with the planning process. A picture paints a thousand words.

Once we establish the blueprint, the idea is to fund that blueprint. How does that work? Here are two examples.

Case Study #1 Pre-Retirees: Meet Ted and Alice

Ted and Alice, a married couple in their early 60s, attended one of my dinner workshops, and took advantage of our free consultation. They brought their Social Security statements, 401(k) statements, IRA statements, and pension statements, as requested, and we had a nice chat. They were nearing retirement, and wanted to make sure they had enough money to retire on, as well as money to travel. Based on that meeting, we agreed to get together again to establish their initial blueprint.

At the next meeting, while Ted and Alice were looking through the numbers, I noticed they started to feel more financially confident as they saw their own buckets unfold in front of them, showing where the money would be coming from and when it will kick in. We walked through it and addressed market risk, longevity risk, and health risk, along with addressing what happens at the death of the first and second spouse. We discussed products that addressed income needs, legacy needs, and asset protection needs, and the tax impact it would have. And lastly, we agreed upon an action plan, and begin implementing it immediately.

In this situation, Ted was eligible for a pension plan, and we concluded that based on his health and age, it made more sense for him to buy private life insurance rather than reduce his pension, so we applied <u>right away</u>, before he retired. We then addressed Social Security and concluded that it was best for Alice to take hers at 66 and for Ted to defer until age 70, since his check was larger. Then we addressed the retirement assets and did a partial "in-service" rollover distribution from Ted's 401(k) plan to a deferred index IRA annuity so that down the road they would have a guaranteed joint lifetime income check to supplement their pension and Social Security. We will also consider Roth conversions on his remaining 401k when he retires to pre-pay his taxes at a lower rate so that he will NEVER have to pay taxes on that money again.

You should have seen the look on their faces. Both Ted and Alice were very pleased with the plan and how it was all laid out on just two pages showing where they are now, what their goals are, and how to get there in a safe, well-thought-out way. Having an action plan really made the difference.

Case Study #2 Retirees: Meet John and Sally

John and Sally were already retired and in their early 70s. They came to a Required Minimum Distribution (RMD) workshop I held on Cape Cod recently. We sold the place out! It was the first time in my career that I had 100 percent attendance from my responders. And what an event it was. We addressed the "Seven Realities of Required Minimum Distributions," a piece you can download from my website at www.fairwayfinancial.net.

As in the earlier case study, John and Sally also took advantage of the free no obligation consultation to get a second opinion on where they stood. We sat down in my office and since they had already made decisions on their Social Security and pension options, we addressed their retirement accounts, mostly IRAs, and a sizable variable annuity that John rolled over from his previous 401(k). So we called the insurance company that issued the annuity directly to find out everything we needed to know about it. Turns out he was paying nearly 4 percent in fees annually. He had an income rider that guaranteed 5 percent per year, but only for purposes of calculating a future income, which would be paid on a joint life basis at 4.5 percent of the income value. And because it was a variable annuity, it was market-based and subject to risk. In other words, he could very well lose all the gains he had made over the previous years as well as his principal. This was no longer in line with what he wanted, which at age 72 was to protect his assets from any downside risk but be able to participate in any upside gain, and take an income in a few more years to supplement his pension and Social Security. Understand that John had done well with this product. He opened it in 2012 with $200,000, and now five years later it was worth about $300,000! However, as we all know with the market, it can go up and it can go down, and now five years older John was more concerned about the safety of his money, and the income it would produce in just a few years. We've all heard of the old adage regarding the market, you buy low and you sell high. So with that in mind, knowing that the market was at an all-time high as of the writing of this book, John thought it wise to take the gains off the table. But he didn't want to have to pay taxes on any of the gain either.

The solution? I found for him a company that would guarantee a higher lifetime joint income, reduce his fees from 4 percent to just 0.95 percent, protect all his previous gains and principal from any direct downside risk, and allow him to have interest calculated on the movement of a market index if the market continued to do well. His response was, "this sounds too good to be true!" After I assured him it wasn't and that I had the numbers and guarantees in writing to back it, he enthusiastically agreed to do a tax-free rollover from his existing annuity to the new one. What was it called? Read on to find out about one of the best kept secrets in the retirement income planning space.

In short, this will provide guaranteed lifetime income during retirement, and transfer what's left at death in one of the most tax-efficient ways possible.

The Retirement Blueprint Summary

So these are the steps:

1. We establish your blueprint.
2. We make any adjustments until you're comfortable with it.
3. We act on it by putting the pieces into place.

You need to fund your income plan. If we determine that a certain vehicle is needed to provide a check for life—whether it's a joint check or an individual check—get it funded. Set the wheels in motion. Put the pieces together according to your blueprint, and then once they're all done, we'll get back together again monitor the plan

For over 30 years, this has been my modus operandi. It's how I have worked with people. It's how I make my own decisions. I get an idea of what I want, I do some research and gather as much information as I can, then I make an informed decision and move on to the next issue. What I do for myself is what I do for my clients. I have my own buckets set up; I practice what I preach.

Actual Case Studies

On the next few pages you will find three cases I did over the last few years that illustrate this process. Names have been changed for privacy but I have used actual numbers.

Case Study #1

Bob and Sue, in their mid-70s, were already retired. They had most of their money in managed accounts even though they were concerned about market volatility and risk. They also wanted to work on home projects and travel while their health was still good.

The Goals:

1. Growth without the direct downside market risk.
2. Address long-term care concerns.
3. Guarantee income for life.

The Solution:

1. Reposition some money into index annuities to provide income and upside potential without any direct downside risk.

The Results for Bob and Sue:

- Growth potential without direct downside market risk.
- Joint lifetime income from security benefit that will double if either Sue or Bob need home health care or long-term care.
- Safer buckets that better address concerns for market risk but allow for upside potential as an inflation hedge.
- A Retirement Income Certified Professional® to coordinate their affairs.

See Bob and Sue's blueprint at right, establishing their buckets and showing current and recommended positions along with their projected cash flows.

RED (Risk) ☐   BLUE (Safe) ☐   GREEN (Essential Toolkit) ☐

Blueprint for Bob (B) and Sue (S)

Current Positions

TIAA/CREF (S)	IRA (B)	CAPITAL ONE	SAVINGS/CHECKING
$750,000	$114,000	$160,000	$12,000
• Eligible to roll over • Fees • Taxable	• Risk • Fees • Taxable	• Safe • Liquid • Emergencies	• Safe • Liquid

Recommended Positions

TIAA/CREF (S)	IRA (S)	IRA 1 (B)	IRA 2 (B)	CAPITAL ONE	BANK
$450,000	$300,000	$150,000	$150,000	$140,000	$32,000
Income Bucket	Income Bucket	Hedge Bucket	Income Bucket	Travel / Projects	Emergencies
• Risk • Fees • RMDs	• Safe • Index gains • LTC Doubler	• Leave as is • Take RMDs • Inflation hedge	• Safe • Index gains • Take RMDs	• Keep as is • Safe	• Keep as is • Safe

Monthly Cash Flow Projections

	TIAA	Soc Sec (S)	Soc Sec (B)	IRA (S)	IRA 1 (B)	IRA 2 (B)	TOTAL
Years 1–5	*3250	1850	1700	0	*600	*600	$8,000
Years 6–10	1750	1850	1700	**2500	600	600	$9,000
Years 11–life	2000	1850	1700	**2500	600	600	$9,250

* Taking systematic distributions to comply with RMD rules based on 3 percent return.
** Based on 5.5 percent hypothetical return. Will double if Sue or Bob need long-term care.

For illustrative purposes only.

Case Study #2

Mike and Jane, in their early 60s, are retiring in one year, and both in good health. Again, most of their money was in three retirement plans at Mike's employer. He was also fortunate enough to have a pension so we had to address which option worked best for them.

The Goals:

1. Develop a retirement income strategy that would protect their money from direct downside risk and provide guaranteed life-time income to supplement Social Security and the pension.
2. Determine the best pension option for them.
3. Create a lifetime income strategy that adjusts for inflation, and has some flexibility.
4. Be able to travel abroad a few times a year.

The Solutions:

1. Index annuities for lifetime income with upside potential, and provisions for addressing nursing home concerns.
2. Purchase private life insurance instead of through the pension plan to maintain control, have a higher income, and replace pension at Mike's death TAX-FREE to Jane.
3. Systematic withdrawals in layers to adjust for inflation.

The Results for Mike and Jane:

1. Growth without direct downside market risk.
2. Guaranteed laddered income for life from IRA annuities.
3. Buckets of wealth to create a better picture of assets.
4. Life insurance on Mike to use as Tax-Free pension replacement.

Footnote: Mike recently retired and received his first income checks from the plan.

See Mike and Jane's blueprint at right, with their buckets established to allow for income, inflation, travel, and emergencies.

Blueprint for Mike (M) and Jane (J)

RED (Risk) ☐ BLUE (Safe) ☐ GREEN (Essential Toolkit) ☐

Current Positions

MONEY PURCHASE (M)	457 PLAN (M)	IRA (J)	ANNUITY (J)	SAVINGS
$550,000	$110,000	$39,000	$21,000	$25,000
• Eligible to roll over • Fees • Taxable	• Risk • Fees • Taxable	• Risk • Fees	• Safe • Deferred	• Safe • Liquid

Recommended Positions

IRA 1 (M)	IRA 2 (M)	FUND ACCT	ANNUITY (J)	IRA (J)	SAVINGS
$300,000	$200,000	$110,000	$140,000	$21,000	$75,000
Future Income	Future Income	Current Income	Deferred Income Accounts		Fun/Travel
• Safe, no risk • 8 percent bonus • Income yr 6	• Safe • Index gains • Income yr 11	• Leave as is • Take income for 60 months	• Keep as is • Index gains only • Take income yrs 6–10	• Keep as is	• Keep as is • Safe

Monthly Cash Flow Projections

	Pension	SSec (M)	Work (J)	SSec (J)	Fund	IRA 1 (M)	A/IRA (J)	IRA 2 (M)	TOTAL
Yrs 1–5	*5360	0	2500	0	2000	0	0	0	$9,860
Yrs 6–10	*5360	0	0	1400	0	**2000	1500	0	$10,260
Yrs 11–life	*5360	3550	0	1400	0	**2000	0	2250	$14,560

* Minus premium of $830/mo for life insurance of $600,000 to place pension.

** Based on hypothetical performance. IRA 1 will double for up to 5 years if Mike or Jane need long-term care.

For illustrative purposes only.

Case Study #3:

Steve (not me!) and Tracy are in their mid-50s, still working and making a good income. Steve did a fantastic job saving money but had a healthy distrust for government sponsored plans and his biggest concerns were future taxes. He was comfortable taking some risk with his money but less as he grew older and needed income. He had no pension and wanted to take Social Security at age 62. He had made good gains in his stocks but didn't want to get too greedy and wanted to sell some now to reposition for future income.

The Goals:
1. Grow money tax efficiently.
2. Provide as much tax-free income as possible.
3. Develop an income replacement plan if Steve should suffer an untimely death in the next 15-20 years or sooner.

The Solutions:
1. Steve was an excellent candidate for Max-Funded Life so we create a tax-free bucket that would provide income for life but also a $2 million tax-free lump sum at death if Steve predeceased Tracy
2. Consolidate his accounts and create buckets to be paid out when they both retire.

The Results for Steve and Tracy
1. Growth potential without direct downside market risk.
2. Joint lifetime income from IRA that will double if home health care or long-term care are needed.
3. Safer buckets that better address concerns for market risk but allow for upside potential and tax-free income.
4. A Retirement Income Certified Professional® to coordinate their affairs.

See Steve and Tracy's blueprint at right, with their buckets established to meet all their goals.

Blueprint for Steve (S) and Tracy (T)

RED (Risk) □   BLUE (Safe) □   GREEN (Essential Toolkit) □

Current Positions

STOCKS	NQ ANNUITY	5 IRAs	2 ROTHs	SAVINGS
$575,000	$400,000	$95,000	$35,000	$300,000
• Risk • Fees • Taxable	• Risk • Fees	• Risk • Fees	• Risk • Fees	• Safe • Liquid

Recommended Positions

STOCKS	MAX-LIFE	NQ ANNUITY	1 IRA	1 ROTH	SAVINGS
$275,000	$500,000	$400,000	$95,000	$35,000	$100,000
Hedge Bucket	Tax-Free Bucket	Tax-Deferred Bucket	Income	Tax-Free	Fun/Travel
• Risk • Fees • Taxable	• Safe • Index gains • x-Tax-Free income	• Safe • 7 percent rollup income	• Risk • Fees • Income	• Risk • Fees	• Safe • Liquid

Monthly Cash Flow Projections

	SSec (S)	SSec (T)	Work (S)	Work (T)	M-Life	NQ Annuity	IRA	ROTH	TOTAL
Age 62–66	*2500	*1500	1000	1000	0	0	0	0	$6,000
Age 67–70	*2500	*1500	0	0	5000	**4000	0	0	$13,000
Age 71–life	*2500	*1500	0	0	5000	**4000	500	0	$13,500

x Income can be tax-free if taken properly. Also, the tax-free death benefit can be used by Steve for chronic or long-term care
* Taking at age 62.
** Will double for up to 4 years if long-term care is needed.

For illustrative purposes only.

Conclusion

NOW THAT YOU'VE READ this far, and have seen how my planning process works from these case studies, I hope that you've decided to get a second opinion to see what's new in the market place that may add value or peace of mind to your existing plan.

Let's recap: The first thing you need to do is gather the information. The internet has made that simpler than it used to be. Gather up the statements from your pension, from Social Security, from your employer-sponsored 401(k) or 403(b) plans, from your IRA, from your brokerage accounts, and from your bank accounts. Most of that information-gathering can be done right on your computer.

Once you have all the information, make that call and sit down with someone like me who can help you put the pieces together in the most advantageous way. The sooner you do it the better, whatever your age—whether you're 50, 55, 60, 65, or 70. The sooner you do it, the more opportunities that you're going to have to make a better plan. The younger you are and the quicker you act, the more opportunities that you have to choose different vehicles to fund your retirement planning.

So gather your assets and make that call. All the knowledge and all the information that I've provided you in this book doesn't matter at all until you take action. You've got to make the call, and you've got to make the time to sit down and plan. You take the time to meet with your doctor. Think of this as a doctor visit for your retirement income. You don't need to take time off from work to do it. I respect your time and your work—I've met with people in my office at 5:00, 6:00, 7:00, and even 8:00 p.m. If it's important to you, then it's important to me.

Sitting down and chatting is extremely important because I know what to ask. We will call your existing account providers; we will get all the facts right. If you have any existing products that you're confused about—maybe variable annuities, mutual funds, or other products—I can help facilitate a phone call to try to get the right answers for you so that you can understand the fees, how they work, and what the risk is. I've done that countless of times with hundreds of clients over the years.

You've taken the time to read this book, now take the next step. Give us a call or visit us on the web at www.fairwayfinancial.net and set up your personalized one-on-one meeting. You'll be glad you did. I look forward to working with you and keeping you on the fairway.

Oh, and be sure to visit the appendix for answers to the quiz, Ten Milestones to Retirement, and Seven Realities of Required Minimum Distributions.

Appendix

Answers to Financial Quiz

1. C
2. D
3. C
4. A
5. C
6. A
7. D
8. False

MILESTONES TO RETIREMENT

As you approach retirement age, it's important to remember your Milestones to Retirement. Use this informative guide as a quick reference throughout your retirement years.

Age	Milestone
50	Up to this point, contributions to your 401(k), 403(b), and 457(b) were capped at $18,000. Now that you are 50 years of age, you may be eligible to put in an additional $6,000 as a catch-up provision to total $24,000. The same is true for your personal IRA. Up until now, the limit has been $5,500. Now you may be eligible to contribute an extra $1,000 for a total $6,500. The annual limitation on catch-up contributions to a SIMPLE-401(k) and a SIMPLE-IRA is $3,000. [1](Contribution limits apply for 2017)
55	Should you separate from your existing employer, you could be eligible to gain access to your tax-deferred savings plan without paying the 10% tax penalty. Check to see if you qualify for one of the exceptions listed in the federal tax code.
59 1/2	Congratulations! In the eyes of the IRS, you're considered old enough to retire and start using your hard-earned tax-deferred money from your retirement plans, such as IRAs and 401(k)s, without having to pay the 10% early distribution tax penalty.
60	Though it could benefit you to wait, you can start receiving widow or widower Social Security benefits at a reduced rate.
62	Depending on your plan and if you're eligible, you could begin receiving your full pension benefits from your employer(s). You can also start your Social Security at a substantially lower rate than if you waited until Full Retirement Age (FRA). This could also affect your spouse's benefit even more.

Age	Milestone
65	At this age, many employers will allow you to access your full pension benefits, and you should be able to qualify for your Medicare benefits as well. For Social Security, you are eligible for full Social Security benefits — unless you were born after 1937.
66	Your birthday will determine your Full Retirement Age (FRA) with Social Security. Eligibility for widow and widower's benefits is based on your birthday — unless you were born prior to 1937.
67	67 is the new FRA for those who were born in 1960 or later. This is the earliest age at which you can claim full Social Security benefits.
70	If you're still delaying your Social Security benefits, delay no more. You have maxed out your Social Security and will no longer receive delayed credits.
70 1/2	At this age, "Uncle Sam" (the IRS) is ready for you to start taking required minimum distributions (RMDs) from many tax-deferred plans so that they can start collecting taxes on those distributions.

[1] https://www.irs.gov/uac/newsroom/irs-announces-2017-pension-plan-limitations-401k-contribution-limit-remainsunchanged-at-18000-for-2017

This information was developed as a general guide to retirement and is not intended as tax or legal advice.

7 REALITIES OF REQUIRED MINIMUM DISTRIBUTIONS

Here are 7 things you should know once you reach the age when you must withdraw Required Minimum Distributions (RMDs):

1. Starting at age 70 ½, you have to withdraw a percentage of money from your retirement accounts based on the previous year's ending values of those accounts. The minimum amount you mustannually withdraw is called a Required Minimum Distribution, and is based on one of two schedules that depend on your marital status and the age difference between you and your spouse.

2. Withdrawals from pre-tax retirement plans can be taxed as current income.

3. If you have remaining employer-sponsored retirement accounts, such as a 401(k) or 403(b), you will have to withdraw your RMD from that account — unlike IRAs, which allow you to choose which account you take the withdrawal from. So, if you wanted to, you could take all of the RMDs from a single IRA. But that's not how it works for employer-sponsored investment accounts.

4. You must calculate your first RMD the year you turn 70 ½. However, the first payment can be delayed until April 1 of the year following the year you turn 70 ½. For all subsequent years, the RMD must be made before December 31. If you delay the initial year's payment of the RMD to April 1, you will still have to take the current year's payment by December 31.

5. If you fail to withdraw your correct RMD amount(s) by the deadline, the IRS has the right to impose a fine of 50 percent of the value you failed to take out, in addition to the taxes on that balance.

6. There are specific RMD rules for survivors taking distributions from spouses' or parents' IRAs.

7. You can make Qualified Charitable Distributions (QCDs) directly from your IRA accounts to a qualified charity and have those contributions count toward your RMD. Monies distributed in this manner are not included in your adjusted gross income.

So, RMDs can be complicated and should be taken seriously.

We provide a detailed retirement blueprint for you and your RMDs to help you avoid mistakes during your mandatory withdrawal period

Fairway Financial does not provide legal or tax advice. Please consult with your attorney, accountant, and/or tax advisor for advice concerning your particular circumstances.

Notes

1. U.S. Department of Health and Human Services. *Long-Term Services and Supports for Older Americans: Risks and Financing Research Brief.* https://aspe.hhs.gov/basic-report/long-term-services-and-supports-older-americans-risks-and-financing-research-brief
2. U.S. Social Security Administration. https://www.ssa.gov/news/press/factsheets/basicfact-alt.pdf
3. Interest calculated based on the movement of a market index, subject to any applicable cap, spread or participation rate.
4. Indexed annuities are insurance contracts that, depending on the contract, may offer a guaranteed annual interest rate and some participation growth, if any, of a stock market index. Such contracts have substantial variation in terms, costs of guarantees and features and may cap participation or returns in significant ways. Any guarantees offered are backed by the financial strength of the insurance company, not an outside entity. Investors are cautioned to carefully review an indexed annuity for its features, costs, risks, and how the variables are calculated.
5. Loans/Withdrawals may reduce cash value and/or the death benefit. They may also cause the policy to lapse. Depending on the status or classification of the policy the withdrawal my not be tax-free. Individuals should consult their financial professional.

About the Author

A graduate of Norwich University, Steve began his insurance and financial planning career in 1986 with John Hancock. As a member of Super Achievers and the Presidents Club, he was among the top five percent of Hancock representatives across the country.

Steven M. Anzuoni, RICP®
Retirement Income
Certified Professional®

In 1999, Steve became an insurance broker and formed Fairway Financial to more objectively serve his clients. Since that time, he has conducted hundreds of financial seminars to address the importance of establishing a more effective retirement planning strategy taking into account Social Security, the impact of taxes, legacy planning, asset protection, and providing lifetime income. He holds his individual and corporate life and health brokers' license in the state of Massachusetts. Steve also holds his RICP® designation from the American College.

Steve is host of *Ready, Set, Retire Radio* on WXTK 95.1 FM on Cape Cod. He has written an article for Forbes.com, been quoted in various financial publications, and has appeared on NECN TV.

Steve resides in Plymouth with his wife Tracy and has two children, Michael and Derek. He enjoys golf, hockey, and serving as a host family to the Bourne Braves of the prestigious Cape Cod Baseball League.

www.ExpertPress.net